Marketi

Martin H. Manser

Chambers Commercial Reference

© W & R Chambers Ltd Edinburgh, 1988
Reprinted 1991

Published by W & R Chambers Ltd Edinburgh, 1988

We have made every effort to mark as such all words which
we believe to be trademarks. We should also like to make
clear that the presence of a word in this book, whether
marked or unmarked, in no way affects its legal status as a
trademark.

British Library Catalogue in Publishing Data
Manser, Martin H.
 Marketing terms.—(Chambers commercial reference series).
 1. Marketing — Dictionaries
 I. Title
 658.8′003′21   HF5412
ISBN 0-550-18066-4

Printed by Singapore National Printers Ltd

Preface

Marketing Terms is a compact but comprehensive reference book which has been specially written to meet the needs of school and college students on a wide range of business and vocational courses at intermediate level.

Along with the other titles in the Chambers Commercial Reference series, *Marketing Terms* provides up-to-date explanations of the key terms used in various areas of business activity. All words and abbreviations are listed alphabetically and defined in clear simple English.

Although intended as a companion to course studies, *Marketing Terms* is also an ideal reference text for those already working in a commercial environment. The book will prove to be an invaluable companion to their work.

Other titles in this Series

Bookkeeping and Accounting Terms
Business Law Terms
Business Terms
Computer Terms
Economics Terms
Office Practice Terms
Office Technology Terms
Printing and Publishing Terms

Marketing Terms

Martin H. Manser is an experienced reference-book editor who has compiled a wide range of reference books and dictionaries.

Aa

à la carte Of the practice in which advertising services are bought from individual suppliers for a fee and only when needed, rather than retaining the services of an advertising agency on a longer term contract.

ABC Abbreviation of **Audit Bureau of Circulation.**

above-the-line advertising Advertising using conventional media such as television, radio, newspapers, cinemas, and outdoor posters. Such expenditure that a recognised advertising agency makes for a client earns the agency a commission. Contrast with *below-the-line advertising*.

accordion fold *(US)* See **concertina fold.**

account The client of an advertising agency, public relations consultancy, etc.

account executive The person in an advertising agency who is responsible for looking after a client's requirements. Also *AE*.

account group A unit within an advertising agency that handles the requirements of a client or group of clients.

ACORN An acronym formed from the words *A Classification of Residential Neighbourhoods*, a type of socio-economic classification that identifies the area and housing in which people live and can be used for direct mail or market research.

adaptation (1) The application of an idea, for example in an advertisement, to other media such as posters and point-of-sale material.   (2) The adapting of an advertisement to a different size or shape.

address line   The part of an advertisement that gives the advertiser's address or the address for inquiries.

addressing machine   An office machine which duplicates information from masters, printing one or a few copies of each of a series of masters. It is used when standard information needs to be duplicated at regular intervals.

adoption   The process by which consumers accept a new product or service. Those who first adopt a new product or service (after the initial interest of innovators) are known as *early adopters.*

advertisement   A paid-for communication aimed at the public or part of it with the purpose of informing and changing public attitudes and behaviour.

advertisement department   The department in an organisation such as a newspaper that is responsible for selling advertising space or time to agencies or to clients directly.

advertisement manager   The person in a publishing company, broadcasting station, etc., who is responsible for selling advertising space or time or poster sites to advertisers.

advertising   The use of paid-for communications aimed at the public or part of it with the purpose of informing and changing public attitudes and behaviour.

advertising agency   An organisation which helps a company to sell its products or services by undertaking market research, creating advertising material, and buying space in newspapers, TV schedules, etc.

advertising brief   A statement of the aims of an advertising campaign, agreed between the client and the advertising agency.

advertising budget   The sum of money allocated for spending on advertising within a given period of time, especially a year. Also known as **advertising appropriation.**

advertising campaign   A planned series of advertisements over a particular period of time.

advertising manager   The person in an organisation who is responsible for planning and carrying out advertising.

advertising medium   (plural *advertising media*) One of the means by which advertising is carried out: the use of newspapers and magazines, television, radio, the cinema, and posters.

advertising rates   The charges made by advertising media for units of advertising space or time. See also **rate card.**

advertising schedule   A plan of the proposed advertising, including details of cost, timing, and the media to be used.

advertising space   The pages or parts of pages in a newspaper or magazine that are available for advertising rather than editorial matter.

Advertising Standards Authority   An independent group established in the UK in 1962 to ensure that the self-regulating system of advertising works effectively in the public interest. The authority handles complaints about (non-broadcast) advertisements. Also *ASA.*

AE   Abbreviation of **account executive.**

after-sales service   The service offered by a seller to a customer following the purchase of goods. Providing spare parts, repairing goods, and advising on the installation and operation of machinery are all examples of after-sales service.

agent   A person who is authorised to act on behalf of another (called the *principal*) in the buying and selling of products and the making of contracts with other individuals and organisations. See also **export agent.**

AIDA An acronym formed from the words *a*ttention, *i*nterest, *d*esire, *a*ction, used as a way of remembering the levels of reaction of potential buyers.

aided recall See **recall.**

air-time The amount of advertising time on radio or television.

aisle A passageway in a supermarket on either side of which products are displayed.

analysis The examination of market research data and information.

animation The creation of the illusion of movement, especially in *animated cartoons*, a film produced from drawings, each successive drawing showing a very slight change of position. A series of such drawings therefore gives the effect of actual movement.

annual A publication, especially a reference book, that is produced annually; year-book.

appeal The element in the message of an advertisement that is designed to meet a particular desire of consumers.

appropriation The sum of money allocated for spending on advertising or sales promotion.

area sampling A technique in which a number of people or organisations within particular geographical areas are sampled at random.

arithmetic mean The result of dividing the total of a series of values by the number of different items in the series. For example, with the values 3, 8, 11, 16, 22, the average is their total (60) divided by the number of items (5) = 12. Also known as **average.** See also **median; mode.**

artwork Illustrations and other graphic material, especially material other than text only, prepared and arranged for reproduction.

ASA   Abbreviation of **Advertising Standards Authority.**

attention value   The degree to which an advertisement has been noticed and remembered by a reader or viewer.

attitude   A personal viewpoint (e.g. 'Buy British') of a product or organisation. Experts differ as to what components attitudes consist of, some considering the constituents to be thought, emotion, and motive, while others consider attitudes consist only of two components: beliefs and values.

attitude research   The investigation of attitudes to a product or organisation by personal interview or group discussion.

attributes   The qualities or features associated with a particular product that are significant to consumers. For example, for cars, the following attributes may be considered important: good performance, safety features, comfort, and luggage space.

audience   The people who are exposed to a particular medium, especially television, radio, or the cinema.

audience measurement   The calculation of the number of people exposed to (advertising on) a particular medium, especially television, radio, or the cinema.

audience research   The discovery of facts, e.g. behaviour patterns and age, about an audience, especially of radio or television programmes.

audio-visual   Of a device or method that uses both sound and vision, e.g. a cassette and filmstrip or slides.

audit   (1) An examination of the financial records of a business and the accounts prepared from them, to verify their accuracy or otherwise. An audit will also normally involve a physical check on stocks and other assets to prove that they actually exist.   (2) See **marketing audit; retail audit; sales audit.**

Audit Bureau of Circulation   An organisation that provides independent certified sales of newspapers and magazines. The UK and USA each has an organisation under this name that provides such information. Also *ABC*.

automatic vending   The sale of products, e.g. cigarettes, confectionery, and petrol, by means of a machine that is operated by the insertion of coins.

average   See **arithmetic mean.**

average cost pricing   A method of fixing the price of a product by adding a gross profit margin on to its average variable costs so as to cover its average total cost of production. This mark-up comprises an overhead element and a fixed net profit margin regarded as normal for the industry.

Bb

back cover (In advertising) the back cover of a magazine, when available for advertising.

banded pack A combination of single products fastened together, e.g. bars of soap or chocolate, offered for sale at a special price or to give one product free.

bar chart A means of representing statistical information in a diagram. Rectangular blocks of varying heights show the actual and proportional quantities of different items.

bar code A printed machine-readable code in the form of vertical lines used on packaging to identify and contain information about a product. Bar codes can be read by a light pen, bar-code scanner, etc. An application is in the labelling of retail products where the light pen is used to record the sale at the time and place of purchase and to control stock. The two most frequently used types are the EAN (European Article Number) and the American UPC (Universal Product Code).

BARB Abbreviation of **Broadcasters' Audience Research Board.**

bargain (1) To make a contract or agreement; to negotiate. (2) A favourable transaction, especially something offered or bought at a low price.

barter The exchanging of products or services without using money.

batch A quantity of items manufactured, stored, or delivered as a group.

Bayesian theory Of a statistical method or theory, used especially in decision-making, in which further information can be added to what is already known about the likelihood of an event, so permitting revisions to be made to previous estimates.

below-the-line advertising Advertising using means other than the conventional methods, e.g. free gifts, point-of-sale material, and direct mail. A commission is not paid to an advertising agency. Contrast with *above-the-line advertising*.

benefit segmentation The separation of a market into groups of consumers who are trying to gain the same benefit from a product.

best-before date The date marked on products, especially foods, to show up to which time the product is in a good enough condition to be used, eaten, etc.

bias The non-statistical errors in a sample survey, caused for example by misunderstanding of questions or not having the correct sample.

bill (1) A statement of money owed. (2) A piece of paper or placard that serves as an advertisement.

billboard (1) (chiefly *US*) A hoarding. (2) A board for a poster of double crown size (30 in × 20 in).

bin A low open container in which packets of products are heaped in a shop, in order to draw attention to a special offer or to gain impulse buys.

binding The (method of) covering that fastens the pages of a book, e.g. by staples, stitches, or glue.

bingo card A business reply card that is bound into a magazine. Numbers are printed as a grid and readers can request information by circling the number that corresponds to the product that is advertised, tearing out the card and returning it to the publisher. Also known as **readers' inquiry card; readers' service card.**

blanket coverage Advertising that is directed at the public in general rather than a particular target audience.

bleed (1) An illustration that extends beyond the trimmed size of a page in order to ensure that the print will run off the page after trimming.   (2) To bleed (or bleed off) is to extend an illustration beyond the trimmed size of a page.

blind advertisement An anonymous advertisement, e.g. by a company in a newspaper in which a box number is used instead of disclosing the advertiser's identity.

blind test The testing of an unidentified new product alongside similar unidentified brands.

blister pack A display packet consisting of a transparent raised covering of clear plastic that is sealed to a backing board and encloses small retail items. Also known as **bubble pack.**

blow up To make a photographic enlargement, the resulting photograph being called a *blow-up.*

blurb A brief promotional description of a book, printed on the jacket or the back of the book.

body copy The main text of an advertisement, excluding the headings and illustrations.

body matter The small type that makes up the main part of an advertisement.

BOGOFF Abbreviation of *buy one get one for free,* a selling strategy in which, on the purchase of one item, the customer receives another free of charge.

bold face A typeface which appears with blacker, heavier strokes than normal and is used for emphasis, e.g. in headings. The entry words in this dictionary are set in bold.

bonus pack A pack that is larger than the usual size but is sold at the normal price of the pack of the standard size.

bonus payment An additional payment, as paid to salesmen, for outstanding achievements.

book token A card bearing a special voucher that can be used in payment or exchange for a book to the stated value.

booklet A short publication that is saddle-stitched and has a limp cover.

booth A stall or stand at an exhibition.

box number A number at a post office or newspaper office to which replies to an advertisement may be sent.

BRAD See **British Rate and Data.**

brainstorming An intensive discussion with the aim of stimulating new ideas and solving problems.

brand The distinctive name, symbol, design, etc., by which a product or group of products is identified.

brand awareness The degree to which potential buyers are familiar with a particular brand or brand name.

brand image The general impression of a particular brand of product.

brand leader The brand of product that has the largest share of the market; market leader.

brand loyalty The support of consumers in continuing to purchase a particular brand of product, rather than buy substitutes or competitive products.

brand manager The marketing executive who is responsible for the promotion and marketing of a particular brand or particular brands of products. Also known as **product manager.**

brand share The proportion of a market in a given commodity that is held by a particular brand of product, expressed in terms of money or units sold.

branded goods Goods that are sold under the proprietary name of their manufacturer.

branding   The creation of a name for a particular product and the firm establishment in consumers' minds of a knowledge of and a continuing commitment to purchase a particular brand.

break   See **commercial break.**

break-even point   The stage in business activity where production and sales are such that total income equals total costs, and neither profit nor loss is made.

breakdown   The division of data into particular categories, for example age, sex, and occupation.

brief   A statement of the aims of an advertising campaign or a marketing research exercise.

British Rate and Data   A monthly publication of advertising rates and mechanical data of UK newspapers and magazines. Also *BRAD.*

British Standards Institution   An organisation which lays down minimum standards of quality for a wide range of manufactured goods. A product carrying the BSI 'Kite mark' is one that conforms to BSI quality specifications. Also *BSI.*

broadcast   To transmit material by radio or television for reception by the public; material transmitted in this way.

Broadcasters' Audience Research Board   The group, established in 1981, that commissions and supervises television audience research in Britain and provides weekly data on television audiences. Formerly known as the *Joint Industry Committee for Television Audience Advertising Research* (*JICTAR*).

broadsheet   Also known as **broadside**   (1) A large sheet of paper that is not folded or cut. The term is commonly used to refer to a newspaper with a large format, approximately 15 in × 24 in (380 mm × 610 mm).   (2) A large single sheet of advertising, printed on one side only.

brochure　A short work, especially one that contains advertising or information, for example one produced by a tour operator giving details of package holidays. Brochures are unbound and saddle-stitched.

broker　A dealer or agent buying and selling (or arranging contracts for others to buy and sell) in insurance, stocks and shares, shipping, etc.

BSI　Abbreviation of **British Standards Institution.**

bubble pack　See **blister pack.**

bucket shop　A small business that cannot always be completely depended upon to fulfil its obligations. The term is used especially to describe a travel agent selling cut-price air tickets.

budget　A financial statement indicating an organisation's planned spending and expected income for a specified future period.

budgetary control　The continual comparison of budget forecasts with actual business performance. This is done in order to try to ensure that the company keeps to its budget, or to find out if the budget itself needs to be revised.

bulk discount　A reduction in a unit price when large quantities are purchased.

bullet　A solid round dot ● used to precede items in a list or to highlight particular points in a text. The bullet is used especially in advertisements and promotions.

bulletin　A report, newsletter, or information sheet issued periodically by an association or organisation.

bulletin board　(1) (chiefly *US*) A notice board. (2) A large outdoor poster or advertising site, especially one that is painted.

bundling　The collecting of different services related to a particular product and the offering of these for sale, in an attempt to make the whole product more appealing. For example, software is often bundled with computers.

bus side   The space on the side of a bus that is available for advertising.

Business Monitors   A series of UK government publications that contain business statistics and are useful, for example, in checking trends in business and identifying developing market opportunities.

business reply service   A postal service which encourages persons to reply to advertising or correspondence at the expense of the original sender. Postage due on the returned cards or envelopes is charged to the licensee.

buyer   (1) A customer or purchaser.   (2) A person who is responsible for choosing and buying goods for shops or industrial companies.

buyers' market   A market in a situation of excess supply. Sellers cannot clear all their output at the prevailing prices and are forced to reduce prices to compete for buyers who are relatively scarce and able to obtain favourable terms.

buying motives   The set of causes that produce a desire to buy something, for example price, delivery times, quality, reliability, brand loyalty, and packaging.

by-line   A line printed with a newspaper or magazine article or photograph that gives the author's or photographer's name.

by-product   A product which comes into existence as a result of the manufacture of another product. For example, sodium hydroxide, used in the production of soap and paper, is a by-product in the manufacture of chlorine.

Cc

call-frequency   The frequency with which a salesman visits customers.

call rate   The number of calls made on customers or potential customers in a given period of time, usually a day or week.

call report   The short written report by a salesman of a visit to a customer or potential customer, to be returned to the sales manager.

calling cycle   The average period of time between calls by a salesman on a particular customer.

camera-ready copy   Graphic material that is ready to be photographed for platemaking by a printer. Also *CRC*. Also known as **camera ready.**

campaign   A series of planned activities designed to achieve a particular aim, especially a planned series of advertisements over a given period of time.

campaign plan   The formal planning of an advertising campaign, including an analysis of the market, a statement of the aims of the campaign, details of how the campaign will be carried out, and plans to monitor the campaign's effectiveness.

canned   (Of a sales presentation) learnt by heart in advance and used with all customers and potential customers.

cannibalisation   The launching of a new product that has a bad effect on the existing sales of another product sold by the same company.

canvass To interview a selected group of people in order to find out their opinions or to sell them something.

canvasser A person who interviews a selected group of people to find out their opinions or to sell them something.

caption (1) The descriptive heading or accompanying wording of an illustration. (2) The heading of an article, section, etc.

captive audience An audience that cannot avoid being exposed to advertising because of its location, e.g. in a cinema.

captive market A market in which there is a sole supplier of a product or service which the customers cannot do without and for which they cannot obtain any acceptable substitute.

carrier A person or business that will transport people or goods for payment.

carrier bag A large reusable bag made of plastic or paper, often printed with the retailer's name or other promotional information.

cartel An association between two or more independent organisations producing the same product. The purpose is to pursue a common policy on controlling prices and production, in order to reduce or eliminate competition between cartel members. The Organisation of Petroleum-Exporting Countries (OPEC) is an example of an international cartel.

carton A packaging box made from thin pasteboard; a container of waxed paper or plastic in which milk, etc., is sold.

cash and carry wholesalers A business that sells goods at wholesale terms to customers, especially retailers and caterers, who pay cash and collect the purchases at the same time.

cash cows Products that generate a considerably greater income than the relatively small costs of retaining their high share of the market. Such products are therefore said to be 'milked', i.e. liquid assets can be obtained easily and continually from them. See also **growth-share matrix.**

cash on delivery A method of trading in which the customer pays the person handing over the goods, who in turn passes payment on to the seller of the goods. Also *COD.*

catalogue A publication containing a list and description of a range of products or services. Some catalogues contain illustrations and also prices.

catalogue buying The purchasing of products selected from a catalogue, the orders being made by post or telephone and the goods delivered to the home. See also **mail order.**

catalogue store A shop in which customers order products from catalogues, the ordered goods being brought out from the stock stored behind the showroom.

caveat emptor A Latin expression meaning 'let the buyer beware': the purchaser is himself or herself responsible for checking the quality of the goods bought.

CCTV Abbreviation of **closed-circuit television.**

Ceefax® See **teletext.**

census An official count of the whole population including such information as age, sex, occupation, number of children. In the UK censuses are usually taken every 10 years.

Central Office of Information A government-funded organisation which provides a publicity service for British exporters, advice on international trade, and an answering service dealing with individual inquiries from businessmen and manufacturers. Also *COI.*

centre spread The centre facing two pages of a magazine.

chain store One of a series of shops, especially department stores, under the same management and located in different places. Products are bought centrally.

channel of distribution The means through which a product passes from the producer to the consumer, for example via wholesalers and retail outlets or via a mail-order house. Also known as **distribution channel.**

charge account An account held by a customer with a retail shop that enables products and services to be obtained without having to pay for them immediately.

chart Information arranged in the form of a table, diagram, or graph.

check-out The cash-desk where the buyer pays for goods purchased in a shop or supermarket.

CIF Abbreviation of **cost, insurance, and freight.**

circular A printed or duplicated notice that is widely distributed.

circulation The number of copies of a newspaper or a magazine that are sold, especially in contrast to the number printed or the number of readers of each copy.

CKD Abbreviation of *completely knocked down,* of the supply of products, e.g. furniture, in an unassembled state, to be put together by the purchaser.

classified advertising Advertising in newspapers and magazines that is typeset by the publisher usually in small type and is arranged according to categories, e.g. 'Situations vacant', 'Personal'. Contrast with *display advertising.*

classified directory A privately published telephone directory which lists local businesses, trades, and organisations in alphabetical order of the trade or profession.

classified display advertising Advertising that is between classified advertising and display advertising in presentation. Classified display advertisements for example have their own border and may contain photographs or company logos.

clearance sale The sale of goods at reduced prices to clear surplus stock.

client A person or company that uses the services of a professional organisation such as an advertising agency or public relations consultant.

clip (1) A short sequence of film. (2) (chiefly *US*) A newspaper cutting.

clipping service A press-cutting agency. See **press cuttings.**

closed-circuit television A television system in which the signal is transmitted by cable to a restricted number of receivers, used for example in hospitals and for security purposes in shops. Also *CCTV*.

closing the sale The point in the sales presentation at which a salesman asks the prospective buyer for an order.

cluster A group of people that have similar characteristics, used in market research in *cluster analysis* and *cluster sampling*.

co-operative An association that has open membership and democratic control, the profits from the supply of products or services being shared amongst the members.

co-operative advertising Advertising in which costs are shared between (national) advertisers and (local) retailers who offer their products or services.

COD Abbreviation of **cash on delivery.**

code of practice The formally formulated conditions under which members of a profession agree to conduct business, for example the *Code of Advertising Practice*.

coding   The giving of code numbers to answers in a questionnaire.

cognitive dissonance   The psychological conflict that arises when an action is taken which is in strong opposition to the person's attitudes or beliefs. For example, a consumer may experience cognitive dissonance following the decision to purchase an expensive new item.

COI   Abbreviation of **Central Office of Information.**

cold call   A call by a salesman on a prospective customer without having made an appointment beforehand.

collating machine   A device used in the production of multiple copies of documents. As documents are copied, a collating machine bundles each document set together in chronological order of copying. In more expensive machines, an attachment for stapling, binding, etc., completed sets is incorporated into the collator.

column centimetre   A unit of measuring and charging printed text, especially advertising in a newspaper or magazine, one column in width by one centimetre in depth.

comb binding   See **mechanical binding.**

commando salesman   A member of a special sales force that aggressively sells a new product into a new market.

commercial   An advertisement on radio, television, or cinema.

commercial break   A period of time on radio or television that is used for the broadcasting of advertisements.

commission   (1) Money paid to a salesman or agent who brings about a sale, usually expressed as a percentage of the price paid.   (2) To assign a particular task to an author, editor, artist, etc.   (3) The discount given to a recognised advertising agency by media owners for purchases by the agency's clients. For example an advertising agency may invoice an advertiser for the cost of a television advertisement of £2000, while the agency will be charged by the television company £2000 less a discount, say 15%, i.e. £1700.

comparative advertising   Advertising in which the performance of one's own product is compared with that of the products of competitors. Such advertising is permitted as long as precisely the same items are compared and purely factual comments are made about the competitors' products.

competition   (1) The action when a firm attempts to win over customers from its rival firms, while retaining its existing customers. It does this through price competition and/or non-price competition. The former involves offering its product at a price lower than those of its rivals. The latter involves trying to increase its share of the market while leaving the price of its product unchanged, by persuading customers of the superiority or advantages associated with its products.   (2) A form of sales promotion in which contestants compete for prizes.

competitive advantage   A benefit that gives a product or company superiority over its rivals.

competitive price   A price for a product or service that is low when compared with other similar items.

competitor   A rival business that offers a similar range of products or services.

complaints department   The department in a business company that deals with complaints from customers about the company's products or services. Often a set procedure is followed which may include laboratory tests of the product and checking when and where the product was bought.

complementary goods   Products which are used in association with each other and so have similar patterns of supply and demand, for example record-players and records.

complete refund offer   The offer by a manufacturer to repay the cost of a product (and often also any postal expenses incurred) in the event of a complaint.

completely knocked down   See **CKD.**

compliment slip   A small piece of bond paper usually bearing the company logo and/or the same information as its letterhead which is used to accompany documents or other items in the post when a formal letter is not required.

computer-printed letter   A general letter printed by a computer printer with a personalised name, salutation (greeting line), and address.

concentrated marketing   The marketing of a product or service in which the company concentrates all marketing efforts on just one part of the market.

concept testing   The checking of the acceptability of proposed products or advertisements before they are produced.

concertina fold   A special fold used for pamphlets in which each fold goes in the opposite direction to the previous one. US equivalent: *accordion fold.*

concessionaire   An organisation with the right to operate a business inside premises owned by another or to be the sole sellers of a particular product in an area or country.

condensed type   A narrow typeface.

conglomerate   A business organisation consisting of a holding company and a group of subsidiary companies, each of which may produce a separate and dissimilar range of products.

consignee   The person to whom goods are delivered.

consignment   (1) The delivering of goods.   (2) The goods that have been (or are being) delivered.   (3) Goods 'on consignment' are goods delivered to an agent by a principal and sold on behalf of the principal. The agent receives commission on the sale and the goods remain the property of the principal until sold.

consumer   The final user of a product or service.

consumer advertising   The advertising of products and services to the general public.

consumer behaviour   The habits of people regarding why they buy particular brands, why they go to particular shops to make purchases, etc.

consumer credit   Loans granted to individuals, especially to pay for consumer goods.

consumer durable   A relatively expensive household product, such as a refrigerator or a piece of furniture, which is not immediately used up but gives service for several years.

consumer goods   Products that have passed through all stages of manufacture, e.g. food, detergents, and clothes, bought by members of the public, in contrast to products bought by companies or other organisations and used to produce something else.

consumer legislation   Laws that give rights to consumers of products and services. See **consumer protection.**

consumer market   The market for consumer goods, in contrast to the industrial market, in which the buyers of products are not their final users.

consumer panel   A representative group of consumers who report to manufacturers or suppliers on their use of a product or service over a period of time.

consumer protection   Various laws have been passed in order to protect consumers against dishonest trading, misleading descriptions, faulty goods, excessive interest rates, etc. These include the Sale of Goods Act (1893), the Trade Descriptions Act (1968), the Fair Trading Act (1973), the Weights and Measures Act (1985), the

Consumer Credit Act (1974), and the Food and Drugs Act (1985). There are also organisations which give help and advice to consumers, for example Citizens' Advice Bureaux and local Trading Standards Offices.

consumer research The study of the preferences of consumers in buying products and services.

consumer sovereignty The extent to which consumers, collectively exercising freedom of choice in a free market, are the dominant influence on the pattern of supply and, in the long run, the allocation of productive resources.

consumer surplus The difference between the price actually paid by a consumer for a commodity and the higher price that consumers would be willing to pay rather than do without that purchase. It is a measure of the benefit received from a commodity in excess of the amount paid for it.

consumerism The protection of the rights and interests of buyers of products and services including safeguarding against defective or dangerous goods and misleading information or advertising.

Consumers' Association An independent body which looks after the interests of consumers. Established in 1956, it tests consumer goods for quality, reliability, usefulness, etc., and publishes reports on the tests in its magazine *Which?*

consumption The act of using products and services for the meeting of needs.

container A box, especially a large box of standard size. Containerised goods can be transported by lorry, train, or ship without having to be unpacked and reloaded at each different stage. Containers are a safe and efficient way of transporting goods.

contest A competition in which participants show their skill, those with the best performance receiving a prize.

continuous research   Studies that are undertaken regularly and often to assess trends, often conducted by an organisation with the information being supplied to different subscribing companies.

contract   A legal agreement between two or more parties, for example an offer of the supply of products or services at a particular price that is accepted by the purchaser.

control group   A group of people that is identical, e.g. in number, age, and habits, to a group taking part in a test.

control question   A question in a questionnaire that is designed to check the consistency with the answers given elsewhere in the questionnaire.

controlled circulation   A publication that is distributed free of charge to individuals in a particular specialist trade or profession.

convenience goods   Goods, especially low-priced products, e.g. crisps or sweets, that consumers buy often and are widely available. Consumers do not mind particularly which brand of such goods they buy.

convenience store   A retail shop that sells food and household goods, is located near customers' homes, and is open from early morning to late evening.

copy   The text (words) of an advertisement.

copy brief   A statement of the aims of an advertisement or series of advertisements, prepared for the person who will be writing the text.

copy clearance   The approval of advertisements by representatives of the media.

copy date   The date by which material to be printed must reach a publisher or printer for inclusion in a particular issue of a magazine.

copy platform   The main theme of an advertisement.

copy test   The testing of the words of an advertisement to measure its effectiveness in terms of readers' understanding, interest, action, etc.

copyright   The legal and exclusive right of an originator of a work, photograph, illustration, etc., to reproduce that work unless he or she gives permission to another. Copyright is regulated by national laws and international conventions.

copywriter   The person who writes copy (the text) of advertisements, promotional material, product literature, etc.

corner   To corner a market is to gain complete (or almost complete) control over the supply of a particular item. This is usually done in order to create an artificial scarcity, raise the price of the item, and in this way increase profits.

corporate advertising   The advertising of a business firm or organisation rather than its products or services.

corporate identity   The overall visual identification of a company or organisation, including its distinctive logo, colour schemes, letterhead, etc.

corporate image   The general impression given by a company or organisation in the public mind.

corporate plan   The wide aims and strategies that a company wishes to follow over a period of time, especially five years.

correlation   The establishing of a relationship between two or more variables, e.g. ownership of a car and the age of the driver.

cost centre   A section of a business for which costs can be charged to part of the costing process. A cost centre can be a person, a piece of equipment, a process, a department, etc.

cost-effective   Providing an adequate return for the amount of money spent, especially when compared with something else.

cost, insurance, and freight   A term meaning that the seller's quoted price includes the cost of the goods themselves, the expenses involved in putting the goods on a ship or plane, the cost of transporting the goods to a port of delivery, and the insurance premiums covering the goods up to this point (after which they become the buyer's responsibility). Also *CIF*.

cost of living index   See **retail price index.**

cost per inquiry   A measure of the average cost of achieving a single inquiry in response to an advertising campaign.

cost per thousand   The cost of reaching one thousand people in a certain category, e.g. viewers, listeners, or readers, using a particular advertising medium. Also *CPM; CPT*.

cost-plus pricing   Of a system of charging in which the price is based on the incurred production costs plus a certain amount of money as profit.

costing   The process of measuring and analysing the cost of a business activity, product, department, etc. Accurate costing is essential to business control and planning.

counterpack   A table-top display box holding small quantities of goods.

coupon   (1) A voucher that can be redeemed to give customers a reduction in price on a particular product or other benefit.   (2) Part of an advertisement that can be cut out and returned to the advertiser with the reader's name and address to request further information about a product or service or to make an order.

cover   Any of the outer four pages of a magazine, usually available for advertising: front cover, inside front, inside back, and back cover.

cover page The front or back cover of a magazine, especially when available for advertising at higher rates than on other pages.

cover paper A strong thick paper, usually coloured, used especially for the covers of pamphlets and brochures.

cover price The retail selling price of a newspaper or magazine.

coverage A measure, expressed as a percentage, of potential customers that have been exposed to advertising.

CPM; CPT Abbreviation of **cost per thousand.**

CRC Abbreviation of **camera-ready copy.**

creative department The part of an advertising agency in which ideas are created and expressed in text and design.

creative group A group of people, particularly in a large advertising agency, who specialise in creating ideas, especially for large consumer accounts.

credibility The quality of being believable, e.g. the degree to which advertiser's claims about a product or service can be believed. The difference between what is claimed or stated and what is actually true is known as the *credibility gap*.

credit (1) When a person or organisation is allowed to have goods or services now and pay for them at a later agreed time, that person/organisation is said to have been allowed 'credit'. (2) An acknowledgement of the organisation or person that has provided an illustration, photograph, etc. Also known as **credit line.**

credit account An account held by a customer or business with a retail shop or supplier that enables products and services to be obtained without having to pay for them immediately.

credit card   A card issued to a person by a bank, finance company, retailer, etc. It enables the holder to buy products and services without having to pay for them immediately. The card-holder spends up to a certain agreed limit, and makes a monthly settlement of all or part of the amount due.

credit line   See **credit** (2).

crop   To cut off or mask the areas of an illustration that are not to be reproduced. *Crop marks* are the guidelines showing which parts of an illustration are not to be reproduced, and are placed outside the area that is to be reproduced.

CTN   Abbreviation of *confectioners, tobacconists, and newsagents,* a group of retail shops.

custom-built   Constructed to the specifications of an individual customer.

customer   The purchaser of products or services.

customer needs   The requirements of a potential customer that have to be satisfied for the maintenance of life or well-being.

customer orientation   The inclination in marketing of serving customer needs as a company's priority, shown for example in the way products may be packaged: in large quantities for trade use and in small quantities for household use. Also known as **market orientation.**

customer profile   A description of a typical purchaser of a product or service showing the significant features, e.g. age, income, marital status, and occupation.

customer service   A department in an organisation or a facility to look after customers, for example providing after-sales service (such as repairs and servicing), dealing with queries on orders, giving advice and information, and following up complaints.

cut-price   (Offering products or services) available at prices below the normal standard rates.

cut-throat competition   Ruthless competition between competing sellers of a product or service in which prices are reduced to such a point that little or no profit is made.

cuttings   See **press cuttings.**

Dd

DAGMAR An acronym formed from the words *D*efining *A*dvertising *G*oals for *M*easured *A*dvertising *R*esults; originally the title of a report by the US management consultant Russell H. Colley in 1961 for the Association of National Advertisers in the USA. The significance of the principle is that the effectiveness of advertising can be evaluated only if the aims of advertising are originally specified.

data Facts and other information, from which observations can be made.

data collection The gathering of information, as for input to a computer.

data processing The handling, sorting, recording, analysing, and interpreting of information by computers. Also *DP*.

Data Protection Act An Act of Parliament (1984) brought into effect to regulate computer data to protect the privacy of the individual.

databank A large collection of information stored in a computer, which can process it and from which particular items of information can be retrieved when required.

database An organised collection of files of information that has been systematically recorded. The files can be interconnected and form the base of an organisation's data processing system, with specific reference to information retrieval.

date coding The stamping on containers, especially food containers, of a date after which the products should not be used.

deadline   The date before which a particular task must be completed, for example the time after which material for an issue of a newspaper or magazine will not be accepted.

dealer   A person or company engaged in trade; one that buys and sells products or services as a retailer or wholesaler.

dealer brand   See **own label.**

dealership   The authority to sell products or services as an appointed dealer. Dealerships are usually concerned with goods that need after-sales service or with goods, e.g. cars, that have limited distribution.

debit card   A plastic card containing coded information that enables money to be directly transferred from a customer's current account to the retailer's account, without the need for cheques.

decentralisation   The transfer of responsibilities and powers from a single controlling authority to individual smaller units, especially in different geographical areas.

decision-making unit   The variable group of people that are responsible for deciding which product to buy. Also *DMU*.

delivery note   A list of goods delivered, given to the customer with the goods, also the document that is signed by the person receiving the goods, confirming their safe delivery.

Delphi technique   A method of forecasting possible future technological trends in which a group of experts each give their own opinion. The results are shared among the experts to inspire creative thinking and to come to an opinion of the possible time-scale of any projected developments.

demand   The quantity of a product or service that customers are willing and able to buy per unit of time at a particular price. It is usually true that the quantity demanded of a product falls if its price increases, and vice versa.

demand forecasting The finding out of what the demand for a product or service will be at various selling prices in order to show the price at which the greatest profit will be made.

demand schedule A table stating, for a given state of demand, the quantity of a commodity per day, week, month, etc., that buyers would be prepared to purchase at each of a range of prices.

demand theory The branch of economics that analyses the determinants of consumers' choice of a particular set of purchases from all those that are available. They include the consumers' tastes and habits, income, and the prices of the products. There is an underlying assumption that consumers, within the limitations imposed by income, seek that combination of products and services that gives the greatest satisfaction.

demarketing The discouraging of consumers from buying or consuming products or services. The UK Government's discouragement of the purchase of cigarettes by printing health warnings on every packet is an example of demarketing.

demography The study of population, especially with reference to size, density, and distribution. The statistics about the structure, etc., of the population are known as *demographics*.

demonstration A practical display of how a product works in order to get people to buy it.

department store A large store, traditionally located in the centre of a town or city, selling a wide range of products in different departments, e.g. clothing and furniture.

depreciation   The (rate of) falling in value of an asset, e.g. plant, machinery, or vehicles, due to wear and tear, obsolescence, or the passage of time.

depth interview   An informal unstructured conversation between an interviewer and respondent, with the aim of discovering hidden motives, needs, etc. The interviewer operates within extensive guidelines and the respondent is encouraged to develop opinions and ideas freely.

derived demand   A demand that exists only as a result of another demand. The need of a firm for each of the various types of productive inputs that it requires, such as employees, land, buildings, machinery, equipment, and raw materials, arises solely out of the demand for the products or services which the firm produces with their help.

design   (1) The arrangement of the form and appearance of a product.   (2) The planning and arrangement, e.g. of typography and graphics, of the visual form of advertisements, printing, exhibitions, etc.

desk research   Research that is carried out by examining existing (secondary) data, e.g. surveys, records, and official statistics.

devaluation   A reduction in the value of a currency as compared with other currencies. It is achieved by lowering the exchange rate, and usually has the effect of reducing a country's imports.

diary method   A research technique in which respondents (members of a *diary panel*) keep a regular written record over a particular period of time of the products they buy or the television programmes they watch.

dichotomous question   A question in a questionnaire that requires a simple answer of 'Yes' or 'No'.

differential advantage   A benefit of a product or service that is perceived to make it more suitable or desirable than a competitive product or service.

differentiated marketing   The marketing of a product or service to provide a slightly different version so as to meet the particular needs of the members of a significant part of the market.

diffusion of innovation   The process by which customers accept new products and services.

diminishing returns   See **law of diminishing returns.**

direct costs   Costs that are directly related to a particular product or task, in contrast to general overhead business costs (*indirect costs*).

direct mail   The sending of promotional material to named potential customers by means of the postal service.

direct mailshot   A single mailing in a direct-mail campaign for a particular product or service, consisting for example of a letter and order form, or a catalogue.

direct marketing   The selling of products or services by the manufacturers or producers directly to the consumer without using a retail outlet. Examples of direct marketing include mail-order selling and telephone selling.

direct response advertising   The method of using advertisements, especially in newspapers and magazines, to elicit a direct response by readers, etc., e.g. by filling in a coupon to order a product or to request further information.

direct selling   A method of selling without retail outlets, wholesalers, middlemen, etc. Traditional examples of direct selling include the door-to-door sale of milk, household items, and encyclopaedias.

directory   A reference book, especially one published regularly, e.g. yearly, with information on different business companies, trades, and organisations, and their range of products or services.

discount   A reduction in the quoted price of a product, often in the form of a percentage, to encourage or increase purchases by a consumer.

discount store   A large retail shop that sells products at reduced prices, because e.g. they buy products in large quantities direct from the manufacturers, they offer minimal delivery service to customers, and they have a purely functional level of decoration.

discretionary income   The amount of income remaining from a person's salary or wages after all regular fixed expenditure on necessary items has been met. The discretionary income therefore represents the amount of money that can be spent on the non-essential products or services that the consumer wants to purchase.

diseconomies of scale   When higher output causes even higher costs. The rise in the average total cost of a unit of its product encountered by a firm beyond some stage of a long-run period of expansion. Expansion of output of x per cent causes total production costs to increase by more than x per cent.

display   (1) The showing or exhibiting of products, e.g. in a shop window.   (2) The presentation of a product or promotional material designed to gain the attention of potential customers.

display advertising   Advertising in newspapers and magazines that includes headlines, different typefaces, etc., and often illustrations, to attract readers' attention. Contrast with *classified advertising*.

display outer   A container used to protect products while being transported that can be converted into a display unit with a panel which folds from the lid for use at the point of sale.

disposable personal income   The amount of income remaining from a person's salary or wages after all income tax, national insurance contributions, and other compulsory deductions have been levied.

distribution   The process of transferring products from producers to consumers, including packaging, transport, and warehousing. See also **channel of distribution.**

distribution channel   See **channel of distribution.**

distributor   A business firm, e.g. a wholesaler or retailer, that sells products manufactured by others. See also **foreign distributor.**

distributor brand   See **own label.**

diversification   An extension of a company's activities or range of products. Companies may diversify in order to grow faster, reduce seasonal trade fluctuations, spread risks, etc.

DIY   Abbreviation of **do it yourself.**

DMU   Abbreviation of **decision-making unit.**

do it yourself   The making, decorating, or repairing of household items oneself, without calling on specialist tradespeople; the supplies and materials needed for such work. Also *DIY.*

dogs   Products that have a low market share and a low rate of market growth. They remain in production mainly for sentimental reasons but are not at all profitable. See also **growth-share matrix.**

dominate   (Of a product or service) to have the most significant share of the total market; to be the market leader.

door-to-door   Calling at each house in an area for the purposes of selling products or services (e.g. cosmetics or insurance) or for canvassing opinions.

double-page spread   The two facing pages of a publication, as used for an advertisement or illustration across the two pages.

down market   (Of products and services) at the cheaper, more basic, lower-quality end of the market.

DP   Abbreviation of **data processing.**

dry-transfer lettering   Lettering on the back of a plastic sheet that can be rubbed down onto paper, etc., when preparing artwork.

dummy   A sample of a proposed package, publication, advertisement, etc., that shows what the finished article will look like, for example in order to find out reaction to its effectiveness.

dumpbin   A low open container in which packets of goods are heaped in a shop, in order to draw attention to a special offer or to gain impulse buys.

dumping   The selling of a commodity on a foreign market at a price below the cost of producing it. An exporting firm, with or without government subsidy, may pursue this policy in order to eliminate competition, to break into a new market, or to dispose of temporary surpluses, without causing a reduction in home prices.

durable goods   Products such as cars, refrigerators, or machines that are not used up within a short time of being purchased but yield service over an extended period of time.

dustbin check   A survey of the purchases by consumers over a particular period of time by recording the used tins, cartons, etc., put into a special bin or plastic sack.

Ee

EAN   Abbreviation of *European Article Number*; see **bar code.**

early adopters   See **adoption.**

ECGD   Abbreviation of **Export Credit Guarantee Department.**

econometrics   A specialised branch of mathematical and statistical techniques used to develop and to test economic theories.

economic growth   The growth and development of a country's economy, as indicated by increased national income, production and investment, higher standard of living, etc.

economic life   The period from the installation of a building, plant, or piece of equipment up to the point when its obsolescence renders it an uneconomic asset to retain, although it has not reached the end of its physical life.

economies of scale   The advantages gained by an organisation through being large rather than small; the reduction of unit costs. For example a larger firm can buy in bulk, obtain discounts, and train its own staff.

economy size   A package that is larger than the normal-sized package, especially one giving better value for money.

editing   (1) (In market research) the checking of survey data, questionnaires, etc., to ensure that they are complete and properly prepared for coding and analysis. (2) The preparation of written text for typesetting by checking spelling, usage, style, etc. (3) The preparation of a film or tape-recording by choosing parts of what has been filmed or recorded and arranging them in a particular order.

editorial publicity Mention given without charge to a product or service in the news or entertainment part of a newspaper or magazine, rather than as a paid-for advertisement.

EFTPOS Abbreviation of *electronic funds transfer at point of sale*; system that allows customers to pay for products at shop check-outs with a plastic card that directly debits their bank account, without the need for cash or cheques. The money is transferred electronically to the shop's bank account.

elastic demand See **elasticity of demand.**

elasticity A measure of the degree of responsiveness of one variable to a change in another. The elasticity of y with respect to x is the percentage positive or negative change in the size of y caused by a 1 per cent change in the size of x.

elasticity of demand The degree of responsiveness of the quantity demanded of a product to a change in its price. When a slight rise or fall in the price of a product or service produces a more than proportionate change in the amount of people able and willing to buy it, demand is said to be *elastic*. When a change in the price causes a less than proportionate change in the amount demanded, demand is said to be *inelastic*.

electronic funds transfer at point of sale See **EFTPOS.**

electronic point of sale See **EPOS.**

embargo (1) A government ban on the importing of certain goods (or goods from certain countries). The purpose of an embargo may be to protect a certain industry, or to put economic pressure on a particular country.

(2) The stopping of publishing of information in a press release, etc., before a certain time.

enclosure   A document or other information sent through the post accompanying a letter.

endorsement   A statement of approval or support, especially by an expert or a famous person, used to make greater the credibility of a message, e.g. in an advertisement.

entrepreneur   A business owner or manager who risks his or her own money, using judgement and ability to make profits.

envelope stuffer   An item of promotional material enclosed with a letter, invoice, statement, etc.

EPOS   Abbreviation of *electronic point of sale*; system in which shop check-outs are equipped with electronic devices that can read coded information, especially bar codes. A light pen is moved across the bar code on packaging or the bar-coded goods are passed over a scanner. Information is inputted into the computer and is used to give up-to-date data and analysis of sales and stock together with purchase orders.

escalation clause   See **escalator clause.**

escalator cards   Advertisements located next to underground escalators.

escalator clause; escalation clause   A clause in a contract that allows for price increases if the cost of materials or labour increases or one that grants a higher rate of payment (especially commission) for increased sales, turnover, etc., by sales staff.

established   (E.g. of a product or service) firmly and widely accepted.

estimate   A rough calculation or preliminary statement of the price of products or services, made by a supplier to a potential customer.

ethical   (1) (Of advertising) decent, honest and informative, not misleading, dishonest or unscrupulous.   (2) (Of a proprietary pharmaceutical drug) only available to the general public on doctor's prescription.

European Article Number   See **bar code.**

ex gratia payment   A payment that is a favour or goodwill gesture, not the result of any legal obligation or contract.

excess capacity   The operating situation of a firm or industry when actual output is below the level at which all its productive resources are fully employed.

excess demand   A situation in which the quantity of a product or service which buyers wish to buy at the prevailing price exceeds that which sellers are prepared to sell.

excess supply   A situation in which the quantity of a product or service which sellers wish to sell at the prevailing price exceeds the quantity which buyers wish to buy.

exchange   (1) The act of trading.   (2) The transferring of the ownership of products, services, or money for other products, services, or money of equivalent value, in the expectation of benefit to both parties.   (3) A market place for the buying and selling of commodities or stocks and shares.

exchange rate   The number of units of one currency that can be exchanged for one unit of another currency.

exclusion clause   A clause in a contract stating that something is not covered by the contract, e.g. certain risks being excluded from an insurance policy.

exclusive   A significant story or illustration in a magazine or newspaper, not made available to other magazines or newspapers.

exclusive agency agreement   A contract made with an agent giving the sole right to sell a product or to sell a product in a certain geographical area.

exclusive dealing   The granting by a manufacturer to a retailer of sole rights to sell a product within a certain geographical area provided that the retailer does not sell or stock any other directly competitive products.

exempt rating   A business, supplying products or services that are classed as exempt supplies by the VAT legislation, is given an *exempt rating*. This means that the business does not add VAT to the price charged for its goods or services, neither is the business able to reclaim VAT paid on its expenses. See also **zero-rating.**

exempt supplies   Products or services supplied by a business which do not require the business to charge VAT.

exhibition   A promotional presentation in which companies provide information about and display their products and services; the public place in which such a presentation takes place.

expanded type   A typeface that is wider than usual, to give an oblong flattened appearance.

experimentation   A method of marketing research in which something, e.g. new packaging or a different price, is tested with people, the results being observed. Variables are systematically changed in order to increase the accuracy of the results.

exploded view   A drawing or diagram of a complex device, building, etc., that shows the internal structure and relationship of the individual parts.

export agent   A person who markets a manufacturer's products in a foreign country under an exclusive agreement, payment being made on a commission basis. The manufacturer distributes the products directly to buyers and receives payment directly from the buyers.

Export Credit Guarantee Department   A government department which insures UK exporters against losses arising from exporting goods. Risks covered by the

ECGD include non-payment by the buyer, the imposing of import restrictions by a foreign government, political problems in the importing country (e.g. civil war), etc. The Department also helps exporters to obtain loans. Also *ECGD*.

export marketing　The marketing of a company's products or services in a foreign country or foreign countries. See also **international marketing.**

export sales manager　The person who directs a company's export agents and representatives and who supervises the processing of orders up to the point of the sending of the products.

exposition　A large international public exhibition or display, especially of industrial products.

exposure　(1) A large amount of publicity given to someone, an event, etc., by television, newspapers, and magazines, etc.　(2) The total number of potential viewers, listeners, readers, etc., of a certain advertising medium.

extended credit　This describes a purchase where the goods become the property of the buyer immediately (as with monthly accounts or mail order). This differs from hire purchase where the goods do not belong to the buyer finally until the last payment has been made.

extended guarantee　Cover for maintenance and service, as in the case of breakdowns on a consumer durable such as a washing-machine, for a period of time beyond the time specified in the manufacturer's original guarantee, available usually at an extra cost.

extrapolation　The forecasting of future trends on the basis of past facts and events.

Ff

face out   (Of books) displayed on a shelf with the front cover facing outwards.

face-to-face selling   The selling of a product or service in which the seller deals with the buyer personally, in contrast to selling by telephone, letter, etc.

facia   The board over a shop or an exhibition stand that bears the shopkeeper's or exhibitor's name.

facing matter   The placing of an advertisement on an opposite page to editorial matter. Also known as **facing text matter.**

facsimile   An exact copy of a document or illustration.

fact book   A collection of information about a product, e.g. information on sales, competition, and distribution, maintained by the brand manager of a company or by an advertising agency.

factor   (1) An agent who possesses and deals in goods on behalf of a principal, receiving commission for doing so.   (2) A person or organisation engaged in the factoring of debts.   (3) One of a number of things that together make up the cause of something.

factor analysis   The method of identifying a fewer number of underlying factors from a larger number of factors in statistical information, especially research on attitudes.

factoring   A financial service in which a debt-collecting agency takes over responsibility for collecting a company's debts. The factors buy the debts from the company at their face value minus an agreed commission and collect them on their own behalf.

fad A fashion that is intense while it lasts but only goes on for a short time; craze.

family brand One name, especially that of the company, that is used to identify the brand names of a range of products of that company. For example, the family brand Heinz in Heinz tomato ketchup, Heinz baked beans, etc.

family life cycle The different stages though which people pass, used to distinguish certain needs, interests, buying powers, etc., and to work out demand for particular products and services. The progression includes: young single dependent people; young marrieds without children; couples with younger (then older) children; couples whose children have left home; retired people; sole survivors.

fashion (1) A type of sales cycle, seen for example in clothing, car design, and other stylish markets, in which a new design is first of all distinctive, then it is copied, possibly leading to mass-manufactured imitations, and then it is in decline, in order to prepare for the next fashion cycle. See also **fad**. (2) A certain style of clothing, hairstyle, etc., that is popular at a particular time.

fast food A type of hot food, e.g. hamburgers or chips that can be prepared and served very quickly.

fast-moving consumer goods Products such as food, drink, and household goods that are in constant demand, have a low unit value, and are sold quickly. Also *FMCGs*.

feasibility study A systematic detailed investigation of a particular project to find out if it is technically possible and if it is desirable from a financial point of view.

feature An article or story in a magazine or newspaper, either one appearing regularly or produced to give especially detailed treatment in a single issue.

fee A single payment made for a particular service, as charged at an hourly rate and excluding expenses.

feedback Response or reaction that is communicated to the originator of an activity or product. Feedback provides useful information for evaluation or guidelines for further development.

field force A group of interviewers who interview respondents near where the respondents live or work. The arrangement of the work of a field force is known as the *field organisation*.

field research The gathering of marketing information from actual and potential customers by means of interviews, questionnaires, etc.

field sales force The team of sales staff selling products or services directly to customers at their premises.

field sales manager The person responsible for directing, supervising, motivating, etc., the sales force in a particular area.

field selling The direct selling of products or services by sales staff to customers in the market, calling on customers at their premises.

fieldwork The gathering of marketing research that involves investigations carried out on a personal face-to-face basis with respondents, e.g. at home or in shopping centres.

filler Material such as an article, illustration, or advertisement that is used to fill space in a column or page in a newspaper or magazine.

filter question A question in a market research survey that is designed to identify the respondents that should be in the survey.

financial advertising The advertising of insurance, building society investments, share issues, etc.

firm (Of a price, quotation, etc.) on terms that cannot be changed.

fixed costs   Any costs that are not affected by the level of production, e.g. rent, rates, and interest repayments.

fixed spot   A television advertisement that is transmitted within a particular break in a programme, for which a surcharge is paid (e.g. 15% or 20%).

flagship   The most important product, project, or service in a group or range of such items.

flash pack   A package on which a price reduction is printed, to try to gain impulse purchases.

flop   A complete failure in business.

flow chart   A diagrammatic way of showing the logical sequence of steps taken in a given task or procedure or the flow of data through a system.

fly poster   A poster fixed on a site for which neither permission has been granted nor payment has been made.

FMCGs   Abbreviation of **fast-moving consumer goods.**

FOB   Abbreviation of **free on board.**

focus group survey   See **group discussion.**

folder   A sheet of paper printed on one or both sides and folded one or more times.

follow up   To take appropriate action, e.g. by telephoning a potential customer after having written him or her a letter, or to pursue an expression of interest, e.g. in response to an inquiry about a product or service.

forecast   To predict possible future sales, performance, etc., on the basis of data concerned with present and past sales, performance, trends, etc.

foreign distributor   A middleman who handles the products of several manufacturers, buying and selling on his own account and having the opportunity to set market prices and choose methods of distribution.

four p's   Product, price, promotion, and place; the main factors of the **marketing mix.**

franchise An agreement in which a retailer (the *franchisee*) is granted by a company (the *franchisor*) the exclusive right to retail certain products or services in a specified area, in return for a payment, e.g. a continuing service fee. The franchisor grants the franchisee use of its trademark, promotional facilities, etc. Franchises also exist between wholesalers (as franchisors) and retailers (as franchisees) and in the UK between the Independent Broadcasting Authority and radio and television companies to produce programmes.

franking machine A machine that prints a postal impression and date on envelopes and also often carries a company's advertising message.

free advertisement An advertisement carried without charge, for example to a charity.

free gift Something given at no cost to the customer; a promotional device designed to increase sales. Free gifts may be included with or attached to a product; customers may have to apply specially for them, enclosing one or more proofs of purchase; or they may be given if customers examine or purchase other products.

free market One in which the forces of supply and demand are allowed to operate unhindered by government intervention.

free on board This term describes a transaction in which the seller of goods is responsible for all transport, insurance, etc., charges until the goods are loaded on to the ship. Also *FOB*.

free sample An example of a product that is given to consumers in an attempt to encourage them to buy the product.

free trade The condition in which the free flow of products and services is neither restricted nor encouraged by direct government intervention through artificial barriers such as tariffs, quotas on imports, or subsidies on exports.

freebie (In informal usage) something supplied free of charge.

Freefone® A service offered by British Telecom which allows a person to contact by phone a firm who will accept the costs of the call. It is usual for firms to quote a Freefone number in their advertising if they have this arrangement with British Telecom. They will then be billed for the calls they receive. These calls must be made through the operator and it is necessary to quote the Freefone number. See also **LinkLine.**

freelance A self-employed person such as a designer, artist, photographer, or writer who pursues a profession without a long-term commitment to one employer but who is contracted to carry out particular assignments for different firms.

Freepost® A service offered by the Post Office which allows a person to write to a firm. The sender of the letter does not need to use a stamp on the letter, providing the word Freepost appears in the address. The recipient of the letter is then charged for the cost of mailing the letter, plus a fee for the facility.

freesheet A local newspaper or magazine that is distributed door-to-door without charge. All revenue comes from advertising.

french fold A single sheet of paper printed on one side only and folded without cutting the top edge so that the printed side of four pages is visible; used for greetings cards.

frequency The number of times one viewer, listener, or reader is exposed to a particular advertisement in a certain period of time. See also **opportunity to see.**

front cover (In advertising) the front cover of a magazine, when this is available for advertising.

Gg

galley; galley proof   The first proof taken after text has been typeset and before it is made up into pages. So called because galleys in traditional letterpress printing are the long metal trays used to hold type.

Gallup Poll   A method of gauging public opinion by questioning suitably distributed sample individuals, undertaken by the American Institute of Public Opinion or its British counterpart. Named after the US statistician George Horace *Gallup* (1901–84).

game theory   The theory concerned with analysing the choices and strategies available in a business conflict in order to choose the best course of action; used particularly in training or selection procedures.

gap analysis   A method of discovering gaps in the market for possible new products, found by checking off consumer wants against qualities of products already available and noting points where these do not coincide.

gatefold   A page that is wider than the other pages and that has to be folded in on both sides. The folded parts of the page open out like a gate.

GATT   Abbreviation of *General Agreement on Tariffs and Trade*; an international agreement made in 1947. Its purpose is to simplify and standardise international trading procedure by providing a code of conduct, and in particular to reduce the general level of tariffs and other trade restrictions.

GDP   Abbreviation of **gross domestic product.**

General Agreement on Tariffs and Trade   See **GATT.**

generic (1) The name of a brand that has come to be used as a general name for that type of product, e.g. *Biro* for any ball-point pen and *Hoover* for any vacuum-cleaner. (2) Not having a trade name. See **generics.**

generics Products sold without a brand name, in plain packaging, and with no promotion or advertising.

geographical concentration The degree to which the market for a particular product or service is limited to one geographical area, e.g. traditionally Staffordshire is associated with pottery.

Giffen good A foodstuff of relatively low quality which forms an important part of the diet of low-income households. Contrary to the normal rule, the demand for such a product increases when its price rises and decreases when it falls. A price rise forces households to reduce their consumption of other foods and buy more of the Giffen good to maintain their basic nutritional level. A price reduction causes the opposite effect.

gift voucher; gift token A printed card that can be used in payment or exchange for buying certain products to the value of the amount shown.

gimmick An unusual device or idea that is used to attract publicity.

give-away Something given free or at a greatly reduced price, especially something offered with a product or service in order to persuade customers to buy that product or service.

global (Of products or companies) having a name that is recognised throughout the world, e.g. *Coca Cola* and *McDonald's*.

GNP Abbreviation of **gross national product.**

going rate The current prevailing price that is being charged at the time for a service or product.

goods on approval   Goods delivered and examined for a trial period before a decision to buy them is made. If the products do not prove acceptable, they must be returned.

goods on consignment   See **consignment** (3).

goodwill   The part of the value of a business that results from its popularity, efficiency, reputation, etc., in contrast to its capital, stock, etc. Normally, goodwill is taken into consideration only when buying or selling a business.

graph   A diagram showing the relation between sets of numbers or quantities, with reference to two axes.

graphics   (1) Designs containing illustrations or drawings.   (2) The visual arts concerned with representation, illustration, typography, printing, etc., on a flat surface and the methods associated with these techniques.

gross circulation   The total sales of a magazine or newspaper before mistakes or the number of unsold copies have been taken into consideration.

gross domestic product   The value of a nation's total output of goods and services produced in one year by factors of production located in the domestic economy, whoever owns them. Also *GDP*.

gross margin   The difference between the selling price of an article and the cost of the materials and labour needed to produce the article. Also known as **gross profit.**

gross national product   The gross domestic product plus incomes of domestic residents received from abroad as salaries, dividends, or interest, minus similar payments made to residents of other countries. Also *GNP*.

gross profit   See **gross margin.**

group discussion   A research method in which a group of people share their opinions on a particular subject, e.g. a possible new product, an advertisement, or the packaging of a product, with the general supervision of a leader. Also known as **focus group survey.**

growth area A region with rapidly increasing industrial and commercial activity, usually resulting from incentives being offered to employers.

growth market A market in which demand for a product is greatly increasing.

growth-share matrix A diagrammatic analysis of a company's set (*portfolio*) of businesses, arranged according to their rate of market growth and their relative market share. The arrangement has four categories: *cash cows* have a high market share and a low rate of market growth; *dogs* have a low market share and a low rate of market growth; *stars* have a high market share and a high rate of market growth; *problem children* (or *wildcats* or *question marks*) have a low market share and a high rate of market growth.

guarantee (1) A legal document in which the manufacturer of a product agrees to compensate the buyer if the product is faulty (or if it becomes faulty within a specified time).   (2) The undertaking in such a document.   (3) A legally binding agreement to accept responsibility for another person's debts or for the results of another person's actions.

gutter The blank space between two facing pages in a book, magazine, etc.

Hh

habit   The behaviour of consumers in which the same product brand is bought time and time again.

haggle   To bargain over the price of a product, the details of an agreement, etc.

half-tone   A photographic process which represents light and shade by dots of equal intensity but different sizes, the image being photographed through a screen.

hall test   A marketing research test in which passers-by are taken to a public hall or room near a shopping centre, for example to test new products or to answer questions about prices, packaging, etc.

halo effect   The tendency to generalise from the perception of one notably good attribute of a product or organisation to an excessively favourable evaluation of every part of the product or organisation.

handbill   A small printed or duplicated notice that is distributed by hand.

handout   (1) An inexpensive leaflet distributed free of charge at an exhibition, etc.   (2) A document distributed to the press or to an audience as part of a presentation of information.

hard sell   Aggressive and insistent promoting, advertising, or selling methods. Contrast with *soft sell*.

harvesting strategy   A plan to reduce the investment in a product or range of products that have a small declining share of the market. Costs are cut, so increasing profits in the short term, and the product, etc., is then withdrawn from the market.

hawker   A person who goes from door to door selling goods.

headhunting   The seeking out and recruitment, especially through an agency, of suitable managers and executives for jobs in a business or organisation, often taking them from rival companies, etc.

headline   The main line of type at the top of a newspaper article, advertisement, etc., usually set in a larger bolder typeface than the main text.

heavy users   Consumers of a product or service whose usage makes up a disproportionately large share of the total. For example, 20% of consumers may account for 80% of the sales of a product.

heterogeneous products   Products which, although belonging to the same general type, have sufficient individual characteristics to make them non-identical in the eyes of the buyers.

hierarchy of effects   The progression that describes the various steps from awareness of a product through to motivation and action to actually buying it. Various different steps have been suggested, amongst the most well known being *AIDA* (attention, interest, desire, and action).

hierarchy of needs   See **motivation**.

high-involvement products   Products, for example cars or package holidays, that are purchased by consumers after much careful thought and effort in comparing prices in different shops, etc.

high-pressure selling   Intense selling activity marked by an aggressive and very strongly persuasive manner, with no concern for the customer's true needs. Contrast with *low-pressure selling*.

hire purchase   A type of contract in which the buyer has immediate use of an article but pays for it gradually over a period of time. The article remains the seller's property until all the payments have been made.

histogram   A statistical graph in which frequency distribution is shown by means of vertical columns.

historical trend   A tendency shown by the performance of a business, product, etc., in the past, used as a basis for forecasting future trends.

hit rate   (In informal usage) the rate at which something succeeds in reaching its target, e.g. the number of door-to-door calls that have to be made before a customer buys a product.

hoarding   A large outdoor board used to display advertising posters, especially by the side of a road. US equivalent: *billboard*.

home audit   Marketing research that is carried out in a sample of homes, in which a systematic study of what products are bought is conducted. Often respondents are asked to keep a diary to keep a regular written note of the products they buy.

homogeneous products   Products which, although produced by different firms, are undifferentiated and identical in the eyes of the buyer. It is therefore of no consequence from which firm purchases are made.

horizontal integration   The amalgamation of firms engaged in the same stage of production of the same commodity.

horizontal marketing   The development of an existing market, in contrast to establishing new markets (*vertical marketing*). The marketing of office computers and word processors to customers with electric typewriters is an example of horizontal marketing.

horizontal publication   A journal aimed at readership in similar types of job but in different industries.

house agency   An in-house advertising agency owned and run by a business company.

house journal   A periodical that a company may produce up to three or four times per year. It gives information and pictures of past events in the company and varied other information of interest to staff and possibly the general public. It is often found on occasional tables in reception areas of companies for visitors to discover something of the company that they are dealing with.

house style   A consistent style of visual presentation of a company or organisation, including its distinctive logo, colour scheme, letterhead, packaging, etc.

house-to-house   Calling directly at houses in an area to sell products or services, to distribute promotional material, to canvass opinions, etc.

household   A unit consisting either of a single person living alone or a group living together. It is an important economic unit when considering the market potential for certain consumer goods, particularly durables, which are sold on the basis of one per household irrespective of the number in the household.

hype   Exaggerated publicity for a product.

hypermarket   A huge self-service store (with a selling area of over 50,000 sq ft) usually situated out of town that sells a very wide range of food and non-food goods and offers extensive car-parking facilities.

Ii

image   The general impression in the public mind given by a business or organisation or its products or services.

impact   The effect of an advertisement or other form of promotion on a potential customer.

impression   One exposure to an advertisement.

impulse buying; impulse purchase   The buying of items without having previously planned to do so or considered the need for them. Impulse buying can be influenced by attractive packaging and strategic display (e.g. next to the supermarket check-out).

impulse goods   Products that are purchased without previous planning or without considering the need for them. See also **impulse buying.**

impulse purchase   See **impulse buying.**

in-store promotion   Sampling, demonstration, and sales promotion of a product inside a shop or showroom.

incentive   A financial reward or a scheme offering a series of rewards paid according to how well employees (especially sales staff), groups, or companies perform. Bonuses, commission, and other incentives are designed to increase productivity.

incentive marketing   The provision of special encouragements as a reason for buying a product or service. Examples of incentive marketing include special offers, prizes, and competitions.

income   The flow of money accruing to an individual, a firm or other organisation over some period of time. It may originate from the sale of products or services, from wages, interest, dividends, rent, or from a gift or a transfer payment such as a grant.

independent retailer A shop that is owned by one individual or company, i.e. does not belong to a corporate chain of shops.

index number A number which shows the change that has occurred in a price, quantity, or value in comparison to the value at a previously agreed base point in time. The value in the base period is usually given the figure 100. For example, the *retail price index* (RPI) shows the increase (or decrease) in the prices of essential household goods consumed by the (average) family. If the current RPI is 150 then it will show prices have increased by 50% compared with the original time point.

indirect costs Costs such as rent, administration, and other overheads that are not directly related to a particular task, in contrast to *direct costs*.

industrial advertising The advertising of industrial and technical products and services that are used by business firms.

industrial goods Products purchased by companies for use in the operation of their business, e.g. raw materials, goods used in the manufacture of other goods, and industrial equipment and supplies.

industrial market The market for industrial goods, in contrast to the consumer market. In the industrial market, the buyers of products are not their final users.

industrial marketing The marketing of industrial goods and services to business companies, organisations, etc.

inelastic demand See **elasticity of demand.**

inertia selling The sending of unrequested products to householders or businesses and attempting to charge for them if they are not returned.

inferior goods   Products of which less are bought by people in higher income-groups because they can afford to consume superior, and hence more expensive, substitutes.

informant   A person who supplies information in answer to research inquiries.

innovation   The developing and introducing of new products or services to the market. The very first people who (experimentally) buy a new product or service are known as *innovators*.

inquiry   A request from a prospective customer for information about a product or service, made in response to an advertisement or other form of promotion.

insert   Printed matter, such as an advertisement, that is placed loosely into the pages of a magazine or other publication.

inset   (1) Printed matter, such as an advertisement, that is bound into the pages of a magazine or other publication.   (2) A small illustration, such as a map, set within a larger one.

institutional advertising   The advertising of a business firm or whole industry rather than the products or services of one firm.

international marketing   The marketing of a company's products or services to consumers in more than one country, especially with the aim of developing a business in foreign countries and the establishing of local manufacturers, distributors, agents, etc., in those countries.

interview   A contact between two people, either face to face or by telephone, in order to gain information, for example in market research. The person who is conducting the interview is known as the *interviewer*, the person being interviewed the *interviewee* (or informant or respondent in research inquiries). See also **sales interview.**

introductory offer   A special encouragement to buy a product or service when it is first launched, especially by offering a price reduction or promotion for a limited period of time.

inventory   A detailed list of a firm's raw materials, finished goods, equipment, furniture, etc., sometimes also giving the value of each item.

invoice   An official document in a business transaction sent by the seller or supplier to the purchaser as a statement of the products or services supplied, a statement of the amount of money due, what discounts are given, the tax due, etc.

island display   A free-standing display unit that contains products for sale in a supermarket, etc.

italics   Type that slopes to the *right,* used for emphasis in the text.

Jj

JICNARS   Abbreviation of **Joint Industry Committee for National Readership Surveys.**

JICPAS   Abbreviation of **Joint Industry Committee for Poster Audience Surveys.**

JICRAR   Abbreviation of **Joint Industry Committee for Radio Audience Research.**

JICTAR   Abbreviation of *Joint Industry Committee for Television Advertising Research*; see **Broadcasters' Audience Research Board.**

jingle   A short catchy tune or song used as part of a radio or television commercial.

Joint Industry Committee for National Readership Surveys   The group, established in 1968 (taking over from the National Readership Survey), that represents advertisers, advertising agencies, and publishers and is responsible for running a survey of national readership. The reading habits of over 28,000 individuals covering over 100 publications are surveyed, using classifications of social grades (see **socio-economic groups**). Also *JICNARS.*

Joint Industry Committee for Poster Audience Surveys   The group, established in 1967, that represents advertisers, advertising agencies, and associations of poster-site owners, to obtain data on the number of times people in target audiences are exposed to posters. Also *JICPAS.*

Joint Industry Committee for Radio Audience Research   The group, established in 1974, that represents advertisers, advertising agencies, and independent radio companies, that commissions and issues regular reports on radio audience research. Also *JICRAR*.

journey planning The planning of the calls of a member of the sales team so as to make the work as effective as possible. Journey planning includes, for example, working out the number of calls, their location and order, and the route to be taken.

judgement sample The selection of a group of respondents based on (non-statistical) criteria that are chosen by an expert as being most suitable for the research being conducted.

jumbo A very large pack of a product (e.g. washing-powder) or the packing of several units of product (e.g. litres of orange juice) together in a single wrapping.

junk mail (In informal usage) items of direct mail, especially when not specifically requested.

justify To adjust the positions of words on a page, distributing the additional space in lines so that the right margin forms a straight vertical and parallel edge to the left margin.

Kk

KD Abbreviation of *knocked down*, of the supply of goods, e.g. furniture, in an unassembled state, to be put together by the purchaser.

key prospects The buyers in a market with the greatest potential purchasing power; the important potential customers.

keyed advertisement An advertisement with a *key*, i.e. a code number or 'department' reference, that is included in an address or on a coupon so that the source of the inquiry or order can be identified.

knocked down See **KD**.

knocking copy The text of an advertisement that unfairly criticises competitive products or services.

Ll

label   A piece of paper on a container that describes the contents of the container, the product's manufacturer, composition, weight, etc.

lamination   The thin transparent glossy plastic coating that covers a book jacket, certificate, menu, etc., to protect it.

landscape   An illustration, book, etc., having the longer sides at the head and foot. Contrast with *portrait*.

launch   The introduction of a new product or service onto the market.

law of diminishing returns   The economic principle that states that while increasing one input in a productive process by small constant amounts (all other inputs being held constant) may at first cause output per unit to increase, after some point the increases in output will become smaller. Ultimately, successive inputs of the variable factor will result in a less than proportionate increase in output. In the extreme, further additions will become counter-productive and total output will fall.

laws of supply and demand   A set of observations regarding the usual interrelated behaviour of market supply, demand, and price.   (1) If, at the prevailing price, demand exceeds supply, the price tends to rise, and conversely when supply exceeds demand.   (2) A rise in price tends to contract demand and expand supply, and conversely with a fall in price.   (3) Price tends to move to an equilibrium level at which demand is equal to the supply.   (4) The greater the increase or fall in price, the greater the expansion or contraction of supply.   (5) For any given price rise or fall, the expansion or contraction in the quantity supplied will be greater the longer the time the market is allowed to adjust.

layout The arrangement, plan, or design of an advertisement, drawing, etc.

lead time The period of time between the initial placing of an order for a product and receiving the product.

leading question A question that suggests or prompts the expected or desired answer. Leading questions should be avoided in market research.

leaflet A single folded sheet of paper, used especially for advertising or promotional purposes.

leasing A contractual arrangement in which the owner of an asset (the *lessor*) allows someone else (the *lessee*) to use it for a certain period in return for payment. The lessee is sometimes given the opportunity to buy the asset during or after its period of use. An advantage of leasing is that it does not require the lessee to spend a large amount of money before receiving any benefit from the use of the asset. Leasing also offers a facility for continued servicing, which is important with complicated machinery, and the possibility of updating the equipment.

Letraset® A type of transfer lettering.

letterhead The official (heading on) notepaper of an organisation which includes the firm's logo (trademark), the name, address, and telephone number, telex code number, fax number, and information legally required such as registered office address (if a company), registration number, and VAT number.

licensing The selling of the right to use a particular trademark, patent, process, etc., in return for payment of a fee or royalty. Licensing operates particularly in countries to which a company could export only with difficulty. The company (the *licenser*) sells rights to a foreign manufacturer (the *licensee*) who bears the risk of producing the company's products in that country.

life cycle   See **family life cycle; product life cycle.**

lifestyle   The way of life chosen by a community or part of a community, including behaviour at work and leisure and also patterns of dress, eating, drinking, etc.

light pen   A device which looks like a pen but has a light-sensitive tip, which is used for reading bar codes. The light pen is moved across the bar code and it interprets the light and dark strips as direct input to the computer.

limp   (Of a binding) not stiff or rigid with boards, especially having a flexible cover made of artificial cloth.

line artwork   Drawings, diagrams, etc., that consist solely of black lines on white and tint areas, with no intermediate tones and so not needing to be reproduced as half-tones.

line block   A relief block prepared from line artwork, for letterpress printing.

lineage   The number of lines in a piece of printed matter. A *lineage advertisement* in classified advertising is one that is charged at a certain rate per line.

LinkLine®   Either of two services offered by British Telecom. *LinkLine 0800* is a service that allows the public to dial a LinkLine number that begins with 0800 directly, not through the operator. The renter of a LinkLine 0800 number, not the caller, pays for all the charges. *LinkLine 0345* allows callers to dial directly a LinkLine number that begins with 0345 for the cost of a local call (at peak, standard, or cheap rate). The renter of an 0345 number pays an additional charge.

list price   The basic, suggested or recommended retail price, as quoted in the producer's or supplier's catalogue or price-list, before discounts, etc., are taken into consideration.

lithography A printing process that uses the principle that water and grease (ink) do not mix. Printing from a flat-image surface, plates are prepared so that the non-printing area attracts water and rejects ink, whereas the printing area accepts ink and rejects water. See also **offset lithography.**

livery The distinctive style of dress or consistent visual appearance of employees, vehicles, communications, etc., of a company. See also **corporate identity; house style.**

local press Newspapers that are distributed in a particular town, borough, etc., and are usually published once a week.

location The site for filming still, television, or cinema pictures outside the studio.

logistics The management of the flow of the different stages of a complex operation, e.g. the handling of raw materials through production to finished goods and then the distribution of goods to customers.

logo; logotype The identifying symbol, design, trademark, etc., of a company or organisation.

long-range plan A plan of the development of a company or organisation for five or more years in the future.

loose insert A printed advertisement placed loosely into the pages of a magazine or other publication.

loose-leaf Having a binding with two or more rings that may be opened to allow perforated sheets of paper to be easily inserted or removed, used in price-lists, catalogues, etc.

loss leader A product in a shop sold at a loss to attract customers, in the expectation that they will also buy other, more profitable, products and so provide an overall profit for the retailer.

lottery A game of chance (not involving skill) in which prizes are distributed to purchasers of tickets chosen by lot.

loudspeaker van/car A van/car that is fitted with a large external loudspeaker and is driven around an area to make public announcements, used in Britain for example to solicit votes for a particular candidate at an election.

low-involvement products Products that are purchased by consumers without much careful thought.

low-pressure selling Selling activity marked by a subtle indirectness, for example by gaining the potential customer's confidence over a period of time, and understanding the customer's true needs, in contrast to trying to achieve a quick sale in *high-pressure selling*.

luncheon voucher A document which can be exchanged for food. A firm sells the vouchers to employers who give them to employees as tax-free benefits. Luncheon vouchers are regarded as one of the 'incentives' or 'perks' offered by employers who have no canteen facilities in expensive inner-city locations.

luxury good A class of products on which consumers spend a greater share of their income as their income rises. If income rises by 1%, the amount of a luxury good that is purchased increases by more than 1%.

Mm

machine-readable code A bar code in the form of vertical lines used on packaging to identify and contain information about a product. Bar codes can be read by a light pen, bar-code scanner, etc. See also **bar code.**

macro marketing Marketing that is set in the context of the whole of a country's economy and social needs. Contrast with *micro marketing*.

Madison Avenue The US advertising industry, from the name of the street in New York City that is the centre of US advertising and public-relations business.

magazine A publication issued regularly, e.g. weekly or monthly, that is aimed at a particular group of readers, e.g. owners of personal computers, railway modellers.

mail order A type of trading in which the customer orders goods through the postal system, after seeing the catalogue or a newspaper advertisement of a mail-order company (a *mail-order house*). Deliveries are made by post, by carrier, or sometimes through a local agent.

mailing list A list of names and addresses that is used in distributing mailshots. Such lists are often stored on computers and are merged with standard letters to produce personalised correspondence.

mailshot A single mailing in a direct-mail campaign for a particular product or service, consisting for example of a letter and order form, or a catalogue.

make-up The arrangement of type into columns or pages, including the insertion of illustrative matter, advertisements, etc.

management (1) The planning, directing, and controlling of a company or activity. Management involves deciding on policies and organising the efforts of individuals and groups so that the policies can be implemented and objectives reached within an agreed budget. (2) The people in an organisation who are responsible for carrying out these tasks.

manual A book that gives precise instructions or information, e.g. an operating manual on a car or a training manual for new employees.

manufacturers' agent A salesperson who calls on customers on behalf of a manufacturer and who works on a commission basis.

manufacturer's recommended price The price that a manufacturer suggests for a product, often used by retailers as a means of indicating their own lower selling price. See also **resale price maintenance.**

margin (1) An amount of time or money allowed for something over and above the amount strictly required. (2) The difference between the buying and selling prices of an item. (3) See **gross margin.**

marginal cost The amount by which total costs are changed if the output is increased by one unit. Only direct costs are taken into account.

mark-up (1) The difference between the wholesale (or buying) and retail (or selling) prices of an item, often expressed as a percentage, calculated by dividing the amount of the difference by the buying price. For example, if a retailer charges a customer £10 for a shirt that the retailer has bought for £5, the mark-up is £5 (the difference) divided by £5 (the buying price) = 100%. The size of the mark-up does not necessarily reflect the amount of profit. (2) An increase in price.

market (1) A place where buying and selling is done. It could be a physical location (such as Smithfield Meat Market in London) or a 'non-physical' location such as the advertisement columns of a newspaper or a particular group of consumers (e.g. teenagers or farmers) that are potential purchasers of a product or service. (2) The amount or nature of demand for a product or service. (3) To buy and sell; to trade.

market demand The total demand for a product or service in a particular period of time.

market leader The product or the particular brand of product that has the largest share of total sales in a certain market.

market orientation See **customer orientation.**

market penetration The degree to which a company tries to gain further sales for its current products in its existing markets by more aggressive promotion, distribution, etc.

market potential An estimate of the capacity of a particular market to buy a product or service at a certain time.

market profile A description of the significant features, e.g. age, sex, social grouping, and lifestyle, of members of a particular market.

market research The branch of social science that uses scientific methods to gather information about markets for products and services. Market research includes studying the size of the market, its potential growth or decline, customer attitudes, competitive products, pricing, packaging, the effectiveness of advertising, and distribution channels. A variety of methods are used to gain this information, including interviews, questionnaires, panels, surveys, and group discussions. See also **marketing research.**

market segmentation The process of dividing a market into identifiable smaller groups of consumers that share common characteristics, in an effort to improve the marketing performance of a product or service.

72

market share   The percentage of total market sales in a given period that is attributable to one business company.

marketer   A person, business company, etc., that is engaged in marketing.

marketing   The British Institute of Marketing defines marketing as: 'The management process responsible for identifying, anticipating, and satisfying customer requirements profitably.' The American Marketing Association's definition is: 'The performance of business activities that direct the flow of goods and services from producer to customer or user.' Marketing therefore includes the following activities: assessing the potential sales of a product or service; converting the potential into actual demand by advertising, packaging, pricing, and other sales-promoting activities; and organising the efficient distribution of products or provision of services to the consumers.

marketing audit   A detailed analysis of the efficiency of the marketing functions of a company.

marketing board   An organisation of producers that is responsible for the marketing of products, especially agricultural products, e.g. milk in the UK, that show little differentiation between different producers.

marketing communications   The communication of promotional messages by means of advertising, publicity, packaging, sales promotion, and, often, personal selling.

marketing concept   The philosophy underlying a business, particularly that the whole organisation should be orientated towards satisfying its consumers at a planned level of profit.

marketing intelligence   Marketing information that is available or obtainable on a particular market, the intentions of competitive firms, technological trends, etc.

marketing mix   The different elements of the marketing process that need to be effectively co-ordinated in the decisions about marketing. The best-known statement of the marketing mix is the *four p's*: product (e.g. choice of brand name), price, promotion (e.g. advertising and publicity), and place (e.g. distribution, storage, sales staff).

marketing plan A written statement of the marketing aims of a company, including a statement of the products, targets for sales, market shares and profits, promotional and advertising strategies, pricing policies, distribution channels, etc., with precise specifications of timescales, individual responsibilities, etc.

marketing research The systematic recording and analysis of all the information needed for marketing purposes; research into the effectiveness of a company's marketing effort. The expression *marketing research* is used to cover a wider range of activities than *market research*, and includes studies of an economy, a market, demand for and sales of particular products, consumers' buying behaviour, competitive products, pricing, distribution, and promotion.

marketing services The marketing activities in a business firm, excluding selling. Marketing research and advertising are examples of marketing services.

mask To cover the areas on the edge of a photograph which are not to be reproduced.

mass media The means of communication, especially television, radio, and newspapers, that reach a large number of people.

mass production Production of very large quantities of identical items, usually by highly automated processes requiring little manual labour.

masthead The name of a newspaper or periodical in the typographical form in which it normally appears; a similar block of information regularly used as a heading.

matched sample A group of people that have the same characteristics (e.g. sex, age, and income) as another group, used as a sample to test products.

matrix   A rectangular arrangement of data in vertical columns and horizontal lines.

MEAL   Abbreviation of *Media Expenditure Analysis Ltd,* an advertisement research service that compiles data on the expenditure of advertisers on the advertising media, especially newspapers and magazines and television and radio.

mean   See **arithmetic mean.**

mechanical binding   Binding by means of a special device such as a tightly fitting plastic gripper, or a plastic or wire coil inserted through holes in the paper, the latter device being useful where it is important that the book lies flat. Such bindings are used for catalogues, price-lists, etc. In **spiral binding** the pages and cover are joined by a wire or plastic spiral coil. In **wire binding** a metal device with looping finger-like parts is slotted through the punched papers and cover. (**Plastic-**)**comb binding** is the equivalent in plastic.

mechanical data   Production details shown on a rate card of a newspaper or magazine giving information on the size of pages, the width of columns, printing processes, etc.

media   (1) Advertising media: newspapers and magazines, television, radio, the cinema, and posters. See **advertising medium.**   (2) See **mass media.**

media buyer   The executive in an advertising agency who negotiates the buying of advertising space or time with media owners.

Media Expenditure Analysis Ltd   See **MEAL.**

media independent   An advertising agency that restricts its services to planning and buying advertising media, not undertaking any creative work, and passing part of the commission to the advertiser.

media owner   An organisation that owns the right to sell advertising to the public: the publishers of newspapers and magazines, independent television and radio companies, and the advertising contractors of outdoor poster sites and cinemas.

media planner   The executive in an advertising agency who formulates strategies concerning the most effective uses of a particular advertising medium in a campaign.

media research   Investigation into the size, sex, age, income, behaviour, attitudes, etc., of the readers, viewers, listeners, and audiences of the various advertising media.

media schedule   A statement of details of the different advertising media to be used in a campaign, showing size, position, timing, costs, etc.

media selection   The choosing of the precise means of advertising a product or service in order to fulfil the advertising aims, by reaching the target audience in the most cost-effective manner.

median   The number in a series of values that has the same number of values below it as above it; the middle number, e.g. 11 in the series 3, 8, 11, 16, 22.

medium   See **advertising medium; mass media.**

merchandising   The correct displaying of products on a shelf; the activity of making a product prominent in a retail outlet and so more likely to be purchased. Sales promotion schemes, free gifts, special offers, and point-of-sale displays are examples of merchandising. The person who carries out the merchandising of products is known as a *merchandiser*.

merger   The joining together of two or more companies to form a single new company.

micro marketing   Marketing that is set in the context of individual business firms. Contrast with *macro marketing*.

middleman   An intermediate trader, e.g. a wholesaler or agent, between a manufacturer and a consumer of a product.

misrepresentation The making of an untrue or misleading statement in an attempt to persuade someone to enter into a contract.

missionary selling Approaches made by manufacturers to develop goodwill with new contacts who are not the intended final purchasers of a particular product and to increase sales. For example, a publisher's sales representative (the *missionary salesman*) calls on college lecturers to inform them of the publisher's new books. The lecturers will recommend the books to their students who will purchase them from bookshops.

mixed economy An economy in which the ownership of the means of production is partly public (nationalised industries) and partly private (individuals and companies).

mobile A decorative structure that is suspended from the ceiling, with hanging parts that move in air currents; used as a promotional device, e.g. in supermarkets.

mock-up A sample of a proposed package, product, advertisement, etc., for testing, market research, and display purposes.

mode The value that occurs most frequently in a sample.

model A representation that tries to explain or demonstrate something, e.g. a mathematical theory that tries to explain the pricing of a product, or a relief model to show the projected appearance of a new building.

money-back guarantee A statement that a full refund of the purchase price of a product will be made to dissatisfied customers. Sometimes the cost of the customer's postage is also paid.

money-off pack A package of goods that is printed to show a special price reduction.

Monopolies and Mergers Commission Under the Monopolies and Mergers Act of 1965 the government set up the Monopolies Commission. It investigated situations in which a merger or takeover resulted in one organisation controlling 25% or more of the market, this being likely to reduce fair competition and operate against the interests of consumers. Renamed the Monopolies and Mergers Commission under the Fair Trading Act of 1973, the commission investigates the behaviour of companies and makes recommendations to the Trade and Industry Secretary.

monopoly   A situation in which a single organisation controls a large proportion (or all) of the market for its product or service. It can then maximise profits at the expense of the consumer, who is unable to turn to another supplier.

monopsony   A situation where only one buyer exists for the product of several sellers, or where one of several buyers is large enough to exert too much influence over the price of a product or service.

montage   The combination of several separate drawings or photographs to make a single composite design.

motivation   The stimulus or drive that tends to cause people to act in a certain way. One of the most widely used classifications of motivations (or needs to be satisfied) is that proposed by the US psychologist and philosopher Abraham Harold Maslow (1908–70) in 1943. He proposed a *hierarchy of needs*: (1) basic physiological needs; (2) safety needs; (3) social needs; (4) esteem needs; and (5) self-fulfilment needs.

motivation research   The study of the underlying attitudes, motives, emotions, etc., of consumers towards buying products.

multi-brand strategy   The practice of a company having several brands in a group of closely related products, e.g. several different brands of washing-powder, in order to gain and keep a higher share of the market than would be possible with just a single brand.

multi-client survey Marketing research that is financed by a group of subscribing organisations.

multi-dimensional scaling A method in marketing research to measure people's attitudes that uses a scale such as $+3 +2 +1 0 -1 -2 -3$, or $1 2 3 4 5$ to show various levels of like/dislike, agreement/disagreement, etc., of a product.

multi-ring binder A form of mechanical binding in which a number of rings placed near one another keep the pages of a book secure.

multi-stage sampling A form of sampling that uses a random selection in a series of successive stages, e.g. every 20th street within 20 electoral wards.

multinational company A large business organisation which has production and/or distribution operations in several countries.

multiple A company that owns many branches and buys products in bulk or centrally.

multiple-choice question (In research questionnaires) a question that is accompanied by several specified answers, one of which respondents are asked to choose.

Nn

national account   A customer that has many branches throughout the country; a large national retail chain.

national brand   A brand that is available nationally, in contrast to an own-label brand or a brand that is available only on a regional basis.

national launch   The introduction of a new product or service onto the market throughout a country in contrast to making it available gradually on an area-by-area basis.

national press   Newspapers (daily papers or Sunday papers), that are distributed throughout the whole of a country, i.e. not locally or regionally.

nationalisation   A policy of state ownership and control of an entire industry or a single firm. It may be undertaken on grounds of ideology as the most efficient and fair method of organising economic activities, to control natural monopolies, or to keep in existence firms who would otherwise have closed down. A *nationalised industry* is one which produces and markets products and services direct to consumers or other producers, but is owned and controlled by the state.

necessity good   That type of good on which a household spends a smaller proportion of its income as its income increases, and on which it spends a higher proportion of its income as its income falls.

need   Something, e.g. food, drink, clothing, housing, that is essential to maintaining life.

negotiation   Discussion of acceptable terms between different groups (e.g. buyers and sellers) before agreeing a contract or course of action.

net price   (1) The price to be paid after taking into consideration any discounts or deductions.   (2) The price of a net book: see **resale price maintenance.**

net profit   The gross profit minus all operating and selling costs.

net weight   The weight of goods minus the weight of any packaging.

network   A system of television or radio stations connected for broadcasting the same programme. If a programme is *networked*, it is broadcast throughout the country, not limited to one local area or region.

new product development   The whole range of activities concerned with conceiving, screening, evaluating, developing, testing, packaging, designing, and launching of new products onto the market. Also *NPD*.

news agency   An organisation that collects news and for a payment sells the reports to newspapers, periodicals, and television and radio companies.

newspaper   A publication issued usually daily or weekly containing news, reviews, features, and advertisements.

next matter   The placing of an advertisement immediately next to editorial matter. Also known as **next-to-reading matter.**

Nielsen index   Any of several marketing research auditing indexes that continually measure the sales and factors influencing sales in retail and wholesale outlets. The indexes include the Food Index, the Confectionery Index and the Cash and Carry Index.

non-durable goods   Products such as grocery items that are used up within a short time of being purchased.

non-luxury good   A necessity good.

non-price competition   A method of trying to increase a firm's share of a market while leaving the list prices of the products unchanged. The firm seeks to attract new customers and retain existing customers through self-identifying labelling, attractive packaging, advertising, a reputation for quality, after-sales services, the introduction of new brands, bonuses, gifts, etc. See also **competition** (1).

non-probability sampling   A sampling technique in which the researcher has the freedom to choose the sample, rather than the choice being made randomly. An example of non-probability sampling is **quota sampling.**

non-profit making organisation   An organisation, e.g. a charity or art gallery, whose aim is to provide useful services to society or promote an activity. Such a club or institution does not exist for the purpose of trading and/or making a profit.

normal good   A product for which demand increases when income rises and for which demand decreases when income falls.

novelty   A small inexpensive decorative item, toy, etc., e.g. a key ring or badge, used to bear an advertising message.

NPD   Abbreviation of **new product development.**

Oo

observation A method of marketing research in which information is collected by researchers noting events that happen rather than by questioning.

obsolescence The going out of date or out of use of a product or service. Obsolescence may be caused by the invention of more efficient machinery or methods. See also **planned obsolescence.**

odd-even pricing The setting of retail prices with a figure ending in a 5 or 9 (e.g. £4.95 and 99p, rather than £5.00 and £1) in the belief that consumers will find the price more attractive.

off-peak Of time on television (or, less commonly, radio) other than peak times, available at much lower rates, because of lower audiences. Contrast with *peak time.*

off-price label A label on a product showing a special price reduction. Also known as **price-off label.**

Office of Fair Trading A government agency set up in 1973 whose duty is to protect traders and consumers against unfair trading practices. It informs people of their rights and responsibilities, pursues traders guilty of breaking the law, promotes fair competition and higher standards of service, and suggests changes in the laws governing trading practices, credit facilities, and consumer protection. Also *OFT.*

offset lithography The process of lithographic printing from a photographically prepared plate using greasy ink. The image is transferred (offset) onto a rubber-covered cylinder and then to the paper, board, etc. See also **lithography.**

OFT   Abbreviation of **Office of Fair Trading.**

oligopoly   A situation in which there are few sellers of a particular product or service, the market being controlled by a small number of companies competing against each other.

ombudsman   The 'Parliamentary Commissioner for Administration', a government-appointed official who investigates complaints against government departments. The term is now also used to describe other officials with similar functions, e.g. in the areas of banking, insurance, and local government.

omnibus research   Marketing research surveys that contain questions paid for by different individual clients.

on-pack   Of a sales-promotion offer, e.g. a price reduction.

one-stop shopping   A huge shopping centre (often operated by the town or city) that offers shops and department stores which sell a wide range of products to meet most shopping needs. Usually extensive car-parking facilities are provided.

open-ended question   A question in a questionnaire to which the respondent is invited to answer freely in whatever way he or she desires.

opinion leaders   People whose advice or opinion on a new product or service has a significant influence on others and therefore on sales of the product or service.

opinion polls   The testing of (changes in) consumer opinions, especially in politics, e.g. before elections.

opportunity cost   The real cost of acquiring any item, considering what has to be forgone in order to do so. Because resources are limited, the choice of one thing involves doing without another.

opportunity to see   The number of chances that an average member of the target audience will have of being exposed to an advertisement in a particular medium over a particular period of time. Also *OTS*.

option   The right to buy or sell something (e.g. products, shares, property) at a specified price, at or within a specified time, whatever happens to the market price. This right can usually only be obtained by payment of part of the price.

Oracle®   See **teletext**.

organisational buying   The purchasing of products by an organisation rather than an individual.

OTS   Abbreviation of **opportunity to see.**

out-of-town shopping centre   A shopping centre that is located outside the traditional centre of a town or city. Extensive car-parking facilities are available at such shopping centres.

outdoor advertising   Poster displays, usually taken with transportation advertising as one of the categories of advertising media.

outlet   A place where products or services are sold or distributed.

outwork   Tasks connected with a company or industry which are done outside business premises, especially in people's homes.

overheads   Amounts that cannot be measured directly as part of the cost of producing a particular product. Examples of overheads are office staff salaries, rent, insurance, heating, and lighting.

overlay   (1) A transparent sheet over artwork, on which instructions are written.   (2) A transparent sheet used in presenting line artwork for colour reproduction, each colour being drawn in black on an overlay.

overmatter   Text that has been typeset but cannot be printed because of shortage of space. Also known as **overset.**

overprint   To print over already printed matter, e.g. adding the name and address of a local retailer to a leaflet.

overproduction   Producing more products and services than the current demand requires.

overset   See **overmatter.**

own label   A product packaged and sold with the name of the retailer, especially a chain of supermarkets or department stores. Own-label goods are usually sold at prices that are lower than the branded alternative products available in other retail outlets. Also known as **dealer brand; distributor brand; private label.**

Pp

packaging The process of preparing products to be transported, stored, and delivered. Packaging protects the product from damage or contamination and has become a part of the product itself. The packaging identifies the product's contents and may also have instructions for the product's use.

packing The wrapping or enclosing of products in paper, containers, etc.

page proofs Proofs of pages, after corrections made on galleys have been dealt with.

page traffic The proportion of readers of a magazine or newspaper who actually read a particular page.

paired comparisons A test in which respondents are asked to state a sequence of preferences for one of two brands or products.

pallet A type of platform on which products are stacked, enabling them to be easily moved with a fork-lift truck.

pamphlet A short unbound publication usually with a soft cover.

panel A representative group of consumers or shops who report on their habits of buying, using, etc., products or services over a period of time.

pantry check A recording of the actual products and brands as found in the home of research respondents.

Pareto principle The fact that a few significant people or things have a relatively great effect. Sometimes referred to as the 80/20 rule, the principle may be seen for example in company sales: 80% of the sales may come from 20% of the customers. Named after the Italian economist and sociologist Vilfredo Frederico *Pareto* (1848–1923).

partnership   A legal arrangement between two or more people sharing the risks and rewards of a business venture. In a typical partnership contracts made in the normal course of business are binding on all the partners; each partner is fully liable for all the debts of the partnership; and there must be no more than 20 partners (or 10 if the business of the partnership is banking).

party selling   The selling of products from the homes of customers (who act as selling agents), each of whom in turn invites friends and neighbours to offer products for sale and earn a commission on sales. Party selling has been popularised by the manufacturers of Tupperware.

pay-TV   A television service, e.g. by cable, that is paid for by making a regular subscription.

payback   A term used in determining the length of time taken for an investment to earn, recover, or pay back the original sum invested.

PD   Abbreviation of **physical distribution.**

peak time   The period of time on television when the greatest number of people are watching, around the middle of the evening. Contrast with *off-peak.*

pedlar   A person who goes about, especially from door to door, selling goods.

peer group   A group of people of approximately the same age, status, etc., and whose opinions and habits are highly regarded by members of the group.

peg   To keep prices at a given level.

penalty   A sum of money which has to be paid by a person or organisation if they fail to fulfil a contract. Details of the penalty are given in the *penalty clause* of the contract.

penetration   The degree, usually expressed as a percentage, to which an advertisement or product has been accepted by or reaches a potential target audience or market.

penetration pricing   The setting of low prices for a product, accompanied by considerable advertising, in order to secure a large market share for a new product as fast as possible.

per capita income   The total income of a particular social or economic group divided by the number of people in the group.

perception   The process of choosing, receiving, applying, and interpreting sensory stimulations, for example a product may, with effective advertising, be perceived as a crispier, safer, etc., product than its competitors.

perceptual map   A representation that identifies consumers' perceptions of particular qualities of products and plots them on a graph.

perfect competition   The relationship between buyers and sellers that exists in the theoretical concept of a perfectly competitive market. The necessary conditions are: many sellers and buyers, homogeneous goods, equal treatment of buyers, no restriction on entry of new sellers and buyers, perfect information, and unrestricted movement of the commodity. These conditions are rarely all present in real-life situations, but they are a starting point for analysing to what extent reality departs from this theoretical norm.

periodical   A magazine or journal issued regularly, for example monthly or quarterly.

perishables   Food or other material which is liable to rapid deterioration.

personal selling   The selling of a product or service in which the seller deals with the buyer face to face, describing the product or service in spoken words, in contrast to selling by mail order, etc.

personalised letter   A general letter printed by a computer printer in which the recipient's name is included in both the salutation (greeting line) and in the main text of the letter.

personality   (1) A famous person in entertainment or sport, used for example to advertise and promote a product.   (2) The qualities that make up a person's character and lead to particular patterns of behaviour.

personality promotion   The promotion of a product or service, in a shop, or from house to house, in which those promoting the products dress in characteristic clothing, e.g. to represent washing-up liquid. Prizes are distributed freely if the advertised product is in the customer's home and if he or she can answer a simple question correctly.

photoengraving   A method of making relief printing plates for a line or half-tone illustration, in which an image is photographed on a plate and then etched by having the unsensitised parts removed.

photogravure   A method of photoengraving in which the design etched on the metal surface is sunk into the surface, not relief.

photomechanical transfer   A method of quickly producing a photographic print or plate by a chemical transfer process; the print or plate produced by this method. Also *PMT*.

phototypesetting   The production of type images on paper or film that is sensitive to electromagnetic radiation by optical means instead of casting characters by a hot-metal process. The composition is usually undertaken by means of a keyboard linked to a computer to set the text to the required typeface, size, etc., and with the appropriate instructions for hyphenating and justifying end of lines.

physical distribution   The process of transferring products from producers to consumers, including packaging, transport, and warehousing. Also *PD*. See also **channel of distribution.**

pie chart   A method of representing data pictorially, in which sectors of a circle (like slices of a pie) represent different parts or proportions of the whole.

piggy-back promotion   A form of sales promotion that 'rides on the back of' another product, e.g. the offer of a free milk voucher with a packet of breakfast cereal.

pilot   Used to describe a trial or experimental survey, study, etc., to discover how successful this is before the full survey, study, etc., is undertaken.

placard   A small poster, e.g. of double crown size (30 in × 20 in).

planned obsolescence   The deliberate inclusion in a product, e.g. a car, of features which lead to deterioration or out-of-dateness before the end of the product's useful life, to ensure future sales.

plans board   A group of senior departmental heads in an advertising agency who meet to discuss new assignments.

plastic-comb binding   See **mechanical binding.**

PLC   (1) Abbreviation of **public limited company.** (2) Abbreviation of **product life cycle.**

PMT   Abbreviation of **photomechanical transfer.**

point-of-purchase display   A special display in a retail outlet, next to the product being promoted, on a counter, etc., showing for example details of price reductions and features of the product.

point of sale   Also *POS*   (1) The place where a sale is actually made in a retail outlet, at a supermarket check-out, etc. See also **EPOS.**   (2) Promotional material, e.g. display units, posters, leaflets, used at this point to attract customers' attention and so gain sales. Also known as **point-of-sale material.**

population (1) The total number of people living in a country, city, etc. (2) The total number of people or items from which a sample is taken for statistical purposes. Also known as **universe.**

portfolio (1) The folder and other items, e.g. display presentations, price lists, in a salesman's kit, used to present information to prospective customers. (2) A collection of investments (businesses, products, etc.) made by a person or institution. See also **growth-share matrix.**

portrait An illustration, book, etc., whose height is greater than its width. Contrast with *landscape.*

POS Abbreviation of **point of sale.**

positioning The placing of a product in the mind of consumers by emphasising certain distinctive features of the product that fulfil defined consumer needs.

post-purchase anxiety The anxieties caused by the decision to buy a new product. See also **cognitive dissonance.**

post-test The evaluation of the effectiveness of an advertising campaign after it has finished.

postal survey Marketing research conducted by post, in contrast to interviews on the telephone or in person.

postcode The combination of up to 7 letters and numbers used to identify addresses in the United Kingdom, e.g. HP21 8PL, EH7 4AZ, used by business companies to designate different geographical areas, e.g. sales territories, or in market research or direct mail.

poster A large advertisement displayed in a public place. The place or position where a poster is displayed is known as the *poster site.*

PR Abbreviation of **public relations.**

pre-empt structure A system of selling air-time for advertisements on television. An advertisement may be bought in advance at a discount but will not be broadcast if another advertiser pays a higher rate for that air-time.

pre-test The evaluation or trial run of a product or advertisement before it is released or launched.

preferred position The place in a magazine or newspaper where an advertiser wants an advertisement to be printed. Advertisers who want a preferred position are charged an additional amount.

premium An amount paid in addition to a standard price, rate, etc.

premium offer A method of sales promotion in which customers are offered the chance of obtaining one product when another product is bought. For example items that form part of a collection may be given away in cereal packets, or products may be obtained by customers sending (with or without payment) proof of purchase of a particular product.

presence The actual audience for an advertisement on television.

presentation The act of putting information to a group of people in a formal or precise manner, often using handouts, diagrams, videos, etc.

press Newspapers, magazines, etc., considered collectively.

press conference A meeting at which a statement is made about a particular event and reporters from newspapers and television companies, etc., can ask questions.

press cuttings Extracts on a particular subject from newspapers and magazines. A business company that collects such extracts for a fee is known as a *press-cutting agency* or *clipping service, agency,* or *bureau.*

press date The date on which material to be printed is to be passed to press.

press relations   The part of public relations that aims at setting up and keeping a good relationship with the press.

press release   A statement that gives information about something of public interest, sent or given to newspapers, broadcasting companies, etc.

press visit   A visit by newspaper, magazine, television, etc., reporters to a company's offices or factory, usually linked with a special event such as the launch of a major new product.

Prestel®   A public viewdata (interactive videotex) system implemented by British Telecom using the public telephone system. Prestel transmits text, pictures, diagrams, and other images on a television screen, providing a public information service which can be used in home and business. It is a flexible form of a computer-based information retrieval system.

prestige advertising   The advertising of a business firm or organisation rather than its products or services.

preview   A showing of something such as an exhibition or film to an invited audience before it is shown to the general public.

price   The amount in money for which something is offered for sale.

price competition   A method of trying to increase a firm's share of a market by giving the products or services a lower price than that of competitive products or services. See also **competition** (1).

price controls   Government imposed restrictions that regulate or forbid price rises in all or some specified products and services, e.g. in a time of high inflation.

price cutting   The offering of products or services at below the usual or accepted price, especially in order to increase sales.

price discrimination Pricing a product at different levels for different markets. This can be made possible by the markets being far apart geographically, or by the markets being divided into separate classes of consumer (e.g. 'business' and 'domestic' users of electricity).

price elasticity See **elasticity of demand.**

price-fixing (1) The setting of prices by the government. (2) An agreement between two or more producers, sellers, etc., to fix the price of a product at a level which is favourable to themselves, especially to the detriment of the buyer. This is usually illegal.

price leader A firm that by changing the prices of its products gives the signal to the other firms in the industry to change their prices.

price level The average level of prices for a particular range of commodities or for all commodities.

price-list A printed sheet that shows the selling price of a company's different products or services.

price-off label See **off-price label.**

price range The complete set of prices between the highest and lowest for types of product produced by a company.

price-sensitive (Of demand for a product or service) responsive to changes in price. A price-sensitive product is one for which demand falls when the price rises.

price war A period in which two or more competing firms successively cut their prices in an attempt to win a larger share of the market or eliminate competition.

pricing strategy The planning of prices, including the setting of discounts, in considering items such as the price of competitive products, manufacturing and distribution costs, the firm's growth and profitability, customer wants, and the elasticity of demand.

primary data   Information that is collected from original sources for a particular research programme. Contrast with *secondary data*.

prime time   The period of the day at which the radio or television audience is the largest.

principal   A person or company that authorises an agent to act on their behalf in doing business deals.

print run   The number of copies of a publication that are printed at a particular time.

private label   See **own label.**

private sector   All commercial and industrial firms in the economy which are not a part of, or agencies for, central or local government.

privatisation   (1) The selling back by the government into private ownership of all or a part of a firm or an industry that had previously been nationalised.   (2) The granting of permission by the government to firms in the private sector to compete with a nationalised organisation in the provision of a service for which the latter had previously been the sole supplier.

PRO   Abbreviation of **public relations officer.**

pro-forma invoice   An invoice that has to be paid before the ordered products will be delivered.

probability   (A measurement of) the likelihood of an event happening.

probability sampling   See **random sampling.**

probe   A further question used to gain additional information in an interview, questionnaire, etc.

problem children   Products that have a low market share and a high rate of market growth, whose future profitability is not sure. Also known as **question marks; wildcats.** See also **growth-share matrix.**

product   Something that is designed to satisfy consumer needs or wants.

product development   The development of existing products in new ways or the development of new products. See also **new product development.**

product differentiation   The establishing of a special 'identity' for one's product, which helps to set it apart from other competing products and to achieve a particular place in the market. Product differentiation can be achieved by distinctive packaging, advertising, the use of brand names, etc.

product elimination   The removal of a product from the market.

product life cycle   The concept, by analogy with the human life cycle, that all products are developed, are introduced onto the market, grow in sales, reach mature (maximum) sales, then decline in sales and finally end their product life. Also *PLC*.

product line   A group of related products marketed by a company.

product manager   The marketing executive who is responsible for the promotion of a particular brand or particular brands of products. Also known as **brand manager.**

product mix   The range of products offered for sale by a company, and the quantities of each to be sold. The product mix is defined in terms of its *width* (the number of different product lines), *depth* (the average number of different products in a product line), and *consistency* (the degree to which the product lines are related).

product-plus   The features of a product that in the buyer's opinion give it an advantage over its competitors.

product positioning   See **positioning.**

product range   The complete set of products that are sold by one company.

product screening   See **screening.**

product testing   The evaluating of a new product, by testing it with sample groups of potential consumers to gauge their reactions to features of the product.

production control   The responsibility of making sure that all aspects of production run smoothly and efficiently. This involves ensuring that there are sufficient materials of the proper quality, that enough products are produced, and that they are of acceptable quality.

production orientation   The inclination in marketing that the manufacture of products is the priority function of a business and selling them to consumers is secondary.

productivity   Total output divided by the number of units of a particular input employed to produce that output. The motive for increasing productivity is to produce more goods at a lower cost per unit of output. For any given resource (e.g. manpower) it is expressed as the number of units of output (e.g. tons of steel) per unit of input (man-hours).

profit   The (amount of) financial gain resulting from a business activity. It is roughly equivalent to total income minus total spending, and is an indication of the success of a company.

profit centre   A department or other organisational unit within a company that is responsible for making a profit from the operations of that unit.

promotion   See **sales promotion.**

promotional mix   The range of promotional methods used by a company at a given time. See **sales promotion.**

promotional price   A lower price for a product than would normally be charged, used when a product is first launched or to increase sales of an unsuccessful product.

prompted recall   See **recall.**

proof   One or more early impressions printed for the purpose of correcting errors.

proof of purchase   A means of proving that a product has been bought, e.g. the coupon from the bottom of a product, used for example when this is sent as one of several such proofs of purchase to a manufacturer to obtain a free gift.

proprietary goods   Products, e.g. medicine, that are made and owned by a company; this means that it is only they that have the right to make them. A proprietary drug is one that is manufactured by a particular company and marketed under a brand name.

prospect   A potential buyer of a particular product or service.

protectionism   The practice of protecting the producers in one's own country from foreign competitors. This can be done by banning certain imports, by imposing quotas, or by taxing imports so that they become more expensive than their domestic equivalents.

prototype   The first or original full-scale operational model of a product, to be tested and used as a basis for improved models to be manufactured commercially.

provincial press   Newspapers that are distributed in a restricted geographical area, especially a region of the country, published daily or weekly.

psychographic   The measurement of the lifestyle, personalities, attitudes, etc., of people, used as a basis for formulating market segmentation.

public limited company   A company having at least two members and having shares which are available to the general public (but not necessarily quoted on the Stock Exchange). It must publish its accounts and must include the words 'public limited company' (or PLC) in its name. Also *PLC*.

public relations The Institute of Public Relations defines public relations as the 'deliberate, planned, and sustained effort to establish and maintain mutual understanding between an organisation and its public'. A public relations executive aims to promote a favourable image of the company in the minds of its customers and others. Also *PR*.

public relations consultancy An outside person or company used by a firm or organisation to advise on public relations or to carry out public relations activities.

public relations officer The executive in a company or organisation who is responsible for planning and carrying out its public relations activities. Also *PRO*.

public sector That section of the economy collectively owned by the public at large at national, regional, or district level, as distinct from that in private ownership. It includes the central government, the local authorities, and the nationalised industries.

public-service (Of non-commercial advertising or announcements) to do with the general well-being of the community, provided by the advertising media at lower rates or for no charge.

publicity Information or activities that are designed to attract the attention of the public, e.g. the favourable mention of the launching of a new product in the editorial part of a newspaper.

publics (In public relations) identifiable segments of the population, e.g. consumers, shareholders, or legislators.

puff Exaggerated praise in a review or advertisement.

pull/push strategies Two methods of transferring products through a channel of distribution. In a *pull strategy*, consumer demand is created by extensive advertising and promotion, thus persuading retailers (and therefore others in the channel of distribution) to stock the particular brand. In a *push strategy*, the manufacturer has to persuade each person or firm in a channel of distribution to stock a product.

punnet A small shallow basket for fruit, especially strawberries.

purchasing The activity which involves buying all the materials, equipment, and services necessary for the smooth running of a business.

push strategy See **pull/push strategies.**

pyramid selling A method of selling by appointing various levels of distributor, each of whom relies upon further agents to purchase batches of goods.

Qq

qualitative research   Marketing research that is intended to understand the attitudes, motivations, behaviour, etc., of consumers. Qualitative research does not contain statistically measurable information (contrast with *quantitative research*) and is carried out for example in group discussions or interviews.

quality control   The ensuring that manufactured goods are of the necessary standard, especially by closely testing random samples of the products prior to sale.

quantitative research   Marketing research in which a sample is tested and the results are expressed in statistically measurable terms, e.g. the proportion of the population that owns a computer. Contrast with *qualitative research*.

quantity discount   A reduction in the unit price of goods when large quantities are purchased.

question marks   See **problem children.**

questionnaire   A prepared set of printed questions, arranged to obtain the relevant information from respondents in the form of answers. The data collected from questionnaires of a survey sample can then be analysed. For the different types of questions in questionnaires, see **dichotomous question, multiple-choice question,** and **open-ended question.**

quota sampling   A non-random sampling technique in which interviewers are instructed to interview a number of respondents with certain specified features, e.g. age, sex, social grade. The sample is selected to reflect characteristics in the same proportion as are present in the whole population.

quotation   A commercial document sent to a potential purchaser from a supplier, quoting the costs of items, discounts available, transport details, any additional charges to be levied, terms of business, and for how long the prices/terms will hold. The acceptance of a quotation forms a legally binding contract.

Rr

R and D   Abbreviation of **research and development.**

random sampling   A sampling technique in which every possible unit has a known (and usually equal) chance of selection. Also known as **probability sampling.**

rate card   A list of advertising charges for different sizes and types of advertisement, including details of mechanical data, published by a media owner.

rating   A measurement of the audience of a television or radio broadcast. See also **television ratings.**

rationalisation   The reorganising of a business activity or industry in order to achieve greater efficiency and profitability. For example, the number of products in a range might be reduced to leave only the most profitable ones in production.

reach   A measurement of the actual number of viewers, readers, etc., that are exposed at least once to an advertisement, e.g. a television commercial, during a campaign, expressed as a proportion of the total potential number of viewers, etc.

reader advertisement   An advertising feature in a magazine that follows the style of the editorial part of the magazine and in which different products are advertised, often with small photographs or line drawings.

readers' inquiry card; readers' service card   A business reply card that is bound into a magazine. Numbers are printed as a grid and readers can request information by circling the number that corresponds to the product that is advertised, tearing out the card and returning it to the publisher. Also known as **bingo card.**

readership The number of people who read a newspaper or magazine, normally greater than the number of people who buy it. See also **circulation.**

reading and noting Research that aims to measure the proportion of readers of a magazine or newspaper that actually read advertisements and pages, used to test the effectiveness of an advertising campaign.

recall Tests in market research that measure how much consumers remember about advertisements. In *unaided recall,* respondents suggest information spontaneously without any guidance. In *aided recall* (or *prompted recall*) respondents are prompted by being shown something associated with the advertisement to remind them.

reciprocal trading A trading agreement in which two business companies buy from and sell to each other.

recognition (1) Used to describe a method of testing the penetration of advertisements in readers of magazines and newspapers. Respondents go through a publication that they have already read to discover which advertisements can be recalled. (2) The official acceptance of a competent, credit-worthy advertising agency by the controlling media organisations, so enabling the agency to receive commission from media owners. See also **above-the-line advertising; commission** (3).

redemption The act of trading in vouchers, coupons, trading stamps, etc., for a particular product or price reduction.

reference group A social group in which the members depend on and influence one another and share a common set of values and beliefs. Examples of reference groups are the family, teachers, lawyers, and yuppies.

registered design A design, consisting of features of shape, pattern, etc. (not relating to function or methods of construction), that is legally registered to safeguard the owner from unauthorised use.

registered trademark   See **trademark.**

regression analysis   A statistical procedure used to measure the association between one dependent variable and one or more other independent variables to formulate an equation that will predict values of the dependent variable.

relaunch   The reintroduction of a product or service to the market. Changes in the product or service or its marketing accompany such a relaunch.

repeat purchasing   The buying of products that are used frequently, especially low unit-value items such as newspapers and bread.

reply card   A card used to reply to an advertisement. Reply cards are usually pre-paid, i.e. the cost of postage is covered by the company initiating the advertisement rather than the customer who sends off the card.

repositioning   The changing of the placing of a product in the minds of consumers, intended to improve the product's performance and profitability. For example, the product may be packaged differently or new features of the product may be emphasised, in an attempt to encourage a different segment of the market to buy it.

resale price maintenance   The setting of a fixed minimum price on an article by the manufacturer, preventing the retailer from selling it below that price. Since the 1964 Resale Prices Act this is now illegal in most cases. An example of fixed prices is the Net Book Agreement, under which net books may not be sold at less than the price fixed by the publisher. Also *RPM.*

research   See **market research; marketing research; research and development.**

research and development   Scientific investigation of materials, processes, and products. The aims of research and development are to make production more efficient, to design better manufacturing equipment, to improve the company's products, to develop new products, etc. Also *R and D*.

reserve price The minimum price which the seller will accept for an article at an auction.

respondent A person who supplies information in answer to research inquiries.

response rate The proportion of people approached, contacted, etc., who actually respond to an inquiry. Examples of response rate are the number of replies per thousand in a direct-mail promotion or the proportion of a research sample that completes a questionnaire.

retail audit An examination of a sample of retail outlets to yield information on sales, market shares, stocks, marketing, etc. Also known as **shop audit; store audit.**

retail price index An index number designed to measure the change in the average retail price paid by households for the range of goods that they buy. It is often referred to as the *cost of living index* and is the base for calculating the inflation rate. It is calculated by choosing an agreed selection of consumer goods, finding the current prices of those items, expressing these as percentages of their prices in an agreed base year, weighting each percentaged price by the average estimated amount that is bought by each household, and then calculating the average of these weighted percentaged prices. Also *RPI*.

retailer The person or business company that sells products to the general public for personal or family use, e.g. through a shop, department store, multiple, supermarket, etc. The retailer is the last link in the manufacturer-wholesaler-retailer channel of distribution.

retailer co-operative A voluntary association of retailers who together buy products in bulk in order to obtain quantity discounts from the producers. See also **voluntary chain.**

retainer A regular sum, payment of which enables the payer to make use of the services of a person or firm whenever necessary.

returns Products sent back to a supplier, usually because they are damaged or faulty or because they are unsold.

review board A group in an advertising agency that meets to consider critically a suggested campaign before it is presented to a client.

ring binder A loose-leaf binder which has metal rings that can be opened to hold perforated sheets of paper, used for example for a catalogue or price-list.

rolling launch The gradual introduction of a new product or service onto the market.

roman (Of type) of the ordinary upright kind, not italic.

ROP Abbreviation of **run of paper**.

rough A rough sketch to give an impression of an advertisement or other material.

ROW Abbreviation of **run of week**.

royalty A payment made to a person for the right to perform music (or publish a book) written by that person, or for the right to use that person's patents, to extract or sell minerals from the person's land, etc.

RPI Abbreviation of **retail price index**.

RPM Abbreviation of **resale price maintenance**.

run of paper An instruction to a publisher that an advertisement is not to be placed in any special position in the publication, but in the first convenient space available, to be charged at the basic rate. Also *ROP*.

run of week An instruction that an advertisement is to appear during a particular week's issues of a newspaper or broadcasts, but not on a specific day, to be charged at the basic rate. Also *ROW*.

run on To continue to operate a printing machine after completing an initial order, e.g. to print additional copies of an advertisement for trade distribution.

Ss

saddle-stitch To stitch, normally with wire, through the back fold of insetted work, a method of binding used for brochures.

sale (1) The act of transferring the ownership of goods, or performing a service, in return for money. (2) A term describing a period during which products are being sold at lower than normal prices.

sale or return A system in which products are supplied to a retailer who only pays for those which he or she manages to sell, provided the unsold products are returned to the supplier within a specified time.

sales agent An independent person or business firm that sells products or services for a company.

sales aid Material that a sales representative can use to support the face-to-face presentation made to the prospective buyer. Leaflets, videos, and showcards are examples of sales aids.

sales analysis (1) The examination and interpretation of a company's sales figures. (2) Information about actual sales presented in the form of tables.

sales audit A detailed analysis and assessment of a company's sales in terms of the products sold, the channels of distribution, the meeting of sales targets, etc.

sales budget An estimate of expected sales over a period of time, including an estimate of the cost of reaching such a level.

sales calls Visits to (potential) customers by members of the sales force.

sales campaign   A series of planned activities with the aim of increasing sales, especially of a particular product, or selling to a particular geographical area or market segment.

sales conference   A meeting of everyone concerned with the selling of a company's products to consider past performance, forthcoming products, targets, etc.

sales contest   A special scheme that offers incentives to sales staff to reach particular targets.

sales drive   A special effort to increase sales in a particular period of time.

sales force   The personnel in a company, especially the sales representatives, concerned with selling the company's products or services.

sales forecast   An estimate of the amount or value of future sales by taking into account past sales, market trends, market research, similar or competitive products or services, etc.

sales incentive   Something, especially a financial reward or a scheme giving a series of rewards offered to a sales representative, wholesaler, or retailer, with the aim of encouraging them to increase sales, productivity, etc.

sales interview   The contact between the representative of a business company and a prospective customer, in which the member of the sales force presents information on the service or product, answers objections, and seeks to close the sale.

sales lead   An item of basic information, e.g. an inquiry in response to an advertisement, that a salesman can use as a basis for contacting a potential customer.

sales manager   The person who directs a company's sales representatives and who is responsible for selling the company's products or services.

sales mix   A statement of the quantities sold and revenue obtained from the sale of the different products or services of a company.

sales orientation   The inclination in marketing that the selling of products is a company's priority.

sales pitch   The planned presentation by a salesman to a buyer.

sales potential   The maximum possible share of a market that is achievable for a given product or service.

sales promotion   All marketing activities that are intended to sell a product or service, especially the activities that exclude advertising, public relations, etc. Examples of sales promotion are free samples, price reductions, competitions, and point-of-sale displays, and also leaflets describing a product, exhibitions, and sponsorship of sporting events.

sales quota   The target that a company expects a salesman to sell in a given period. Also known as **sales target.**

sales report   A report made by a salesman to a sales manager analysing sales performance and the results of calls made.

sales representative   The person who represents the company in a sales capacity and negotiates, with potential and existing customers, sales offers in the name of the company, especially in a particular geographical territory.

sales revenue   The amount of money received by a company for products or services sold; turnover.

sales target   See **sales quota.**

sales territory   A particular geographical area or part of the market that is assigned to a salesman to sell the company's products or services in.

salesman   Also known as **salesperson;** (*feminine*) **saleswoman**   (1) A person who sells goods in a shop or store.   (2) A sales representative.

112

sample (1) An example of a product that is given to consumers in an attempt to persuade them to buy the product. (2) A limited group of people chosen to be representative of a larger group (known as the *population* or *universe*).

sampling (1) The process of choosing a limited group of people as representative of a larger group. (2) (*US*) The free distribution of examples of a product to consumers in an attempt to persuade them to buy the product.

sampling fraction The proportion of the group (the *population* or *universe*) that is to be sampled.

sampling frame The information that defines the group (the *population* or *universe*) that is to be sampled.

sampling point A convenient geographical location at which sampling is done, e.g. outside a major department store.

sandwich board One of two advertisement boards hung over the shoulders of someone who walks round the streets. One board hangs at the front, the other at the back.

sans serif A style of typeface without serifs.

saturation advertising An overwhelming concentration of advertising, especially for the introduction of a new product or service or to vie with a competitive product.

saturation point A level beyond which the sale of a product or service is not expected or able to increase.

SBU Abbreviation of **strategic business unit**.

scaling (In marketing research) the ranking of items to show the strength of a respondent's attitudes towards a subject.

scc Abbreviation of **single-column centimetre**.

scenario A projected or imagined sequence of events, with an identification of the different factors that might lead to that state of affairs, used in technological forecasting.

screening The process by which a new product idea is systematically checked against certain factors to see if the product is viable.

sealed-bid tendering A method of bidding for orders or contracts in which prospective suppliers put their bid in a sealed envelope. All the offers are opened together at a particular time and the most favourable one is accepted.

secondary data Information that is already available, e.g. government statistics and company records, for use in marketing research. Contrast with *primary data*.

secondary readership Readership that is additional to the person who subscribes to or buys a magazine, e.g. other members of the family or work colleagues.

segmentation The process of dividing a market into identifiable smaller groups of consumers that share common characteristics, in an effort to improve the marketing performance of a product or service.

selective distribution The use of several major stockists for a product, where an unlimited number of stockists is not required. See also **dealership.**

self-liquidating offer A type of sales promotion in which an additional product is offered at a price that covers the costs of its promotion. (The product is made available when customers send in a proof of purchase of another product.)

self-mailer An advertisement sent to a person which includes a postage-paid reply that can be torn off and sent back, i.e. no envelope or special wrapper is needed.

self-service (Of trading, shops, cafeterias, etc.) in which customers themselves select products directly and pay for them at a check-out.

sell-by date The date marked on products, especially foods, to show the date that they should be sold by and beyond which they are no longer fit to be used, eaten, etc.

seller's market A situation in which demand is greater than supply, allowing sellers to increase their prices.

selling See **personal selling.**

semi-display advertising Advertising in the classified section of newspapers and magazines that is typeset by the publisher and uses bolder typefaces, lines of type of different widths, lines above and below the advertisement, etc.

semi-solus An advertisement that appears on a newspaper or magazine page which contains other advertising matter but not immediately next to it.

semi-structured (Of an interview) containing a set of standard questions but allowing the interviewer the freedom and flexibility to ask different or supplementary questions.

seminar A group meeting to discuss a subject or to exchange information.

sequential sampling The analysis of survey research findings as they are received. If the results are repetitive, the survey will not be continued. If further information is needed, additional interviews can be arranged.

serif The finishing stroke at the top and bottom of a printed letter or character.

service Something that is of benefit to an individual or organisation and can be bought or sold. Unlike manufactured products, services cannot be touched (e.g. the services of a solicitor), cannot be separated from their source (e.g. the extraction of a tooth does not exist apart from a dentist), have a short-lived utility (e.g. a reserved seat on a certain train), and are designed for particular needs (e.g. an individual insurance policy).

service charge (1) A proportion (e.g. 10%) of a bill at a restaurant or hotel, which is added to the total instead of the payment of a tip. (2) A sum of money paid by residents of a group of houses, block of flats, etc., for certain services, such as mowing the lawns or cleaning communal areas.

service department The department in a company concerned with after-sales service, e.g. the repairing of faulty goods.

service industry An industry involved in providing a service rather than a manufactured product. Tourism, banking, advertising, and insurance are all service industries.

shelf life The period of time that a product, e.g. packaged food, may be stored or displayed in a shop, etc., without deterioration.

shelf talker A prominent card promoting a product in a shop, positioned on the shelf where the product is displayed. Also known as **shelf wobbler.**

shop audit See **retail audit.**

shoplifting Stealing displayed goods from a shop.

shopping bag A reusable carrier bag made of plastic or paper, often printed with the retailer's name or other promotional information.

shopping centre An area in which a number of different shops are concentrated closely together. A *shopping precinct* is a shopping centre that allows only pedestrian movement and has car-parking facilities.

shopping goods Consumer products over which customers take thought in purchasing, e.g. by shopping around to compare prices and quality. Shoes, washing-machines, and furniture are examples of shopping goods.

shout A bold prominently displayed statement describing a book, printed for example on the book's cover.

showcard A point-of-sale display, advertising products. It is generally placed on a table or sales counter.

shrink-wrap To wrap a product in a transparent protective plastic film that shrinks when heated to produce a closely sealed pack which is suitable for display.

shrinkage The loss of goods in a retail outlet especially by shoplifting, but also by damage or deterioration.

SIC Abbreviation of **Standard Industrial Classification.**

simulation The use of a mathematical procedure, e.g. a computer program, to model the behaviour of a system or process, used for example in marketing research to test the results of adopting different advertising media.

single-column centimetre A unit of measure of advertising in a newspaper, one column in width by one centimetre in depth. Also *scc.*

skew (Of statistics or a curve representing them) not symmetrical about the mean.

skimming pricing The setting of a high price for a new product, in order to appeal to higher-income groups, so 'skimming the cream' from the market.

slogan An advertising catch-phrase that is associated with a particular product or service.

small order An order that is of insufficient value to justify the handling costs. Sometimes a supplier imposes a surcharge for such an order.

social grades See **socio-economic groups.**

social marketing The application of marketing to non-commercial organisations and activities, e.g. those associated with public and social services and also social issues such as the wearing of seat belts or the banning of some aerosol products.

socio-economic groups Divisions of population according to social and economic factors, especially occupation and income. The groups are assigned letters and range from A ('upper-middle class', higher managerial, administrative, and professional positions) through B ('middle class', middle managerial, administrative, and professional positions), C1 ('lower middle class', junior management, supervisory and clerical positions), C2 ('skilled working class', skilled manual positions), D ('working class', semi skilled and unskilled positions), to E (pensioners; lowest paid workers). Also known as **social grades.**

soft goods Textile fabrics and articles made from textile fabrics.

soft sell Promoting, advertising, and selling a product using suggestion and mild persuasion rather than more aggressive insistent tactics (*hard sell*).

sole trader A person who owns and controls his or her own business. A sole trader is not responsible to partners or shareholders, provides the capital to run the business, and is personally liable for the debts which the business may incur.

solus position Of an advertisement in a magazine or newspaper that does not have another advertisement directly next to it.

solus site A poster site on which a poster does not have another poster directly next to it.

space See **advertising space.**

special position A particular location for an advertisement in a magazine or newspaper, e.g. on the front cover, solus (with no other advertisement next to it), and next matter. A higher charge is made for placing advertisements in special positions.

speciality goods (1) Products that have particular features for which consumers will make a special buying effort, e.g. particular brands of cameras. (2) Products and services that are sold direct to customers, not via conventional retail outlets, e.g. encyclopaedias, double glazing, and insurance.

spin-off A by-product of some industrial process or technological development, e.g. non-stick frying-pans were a spin-off from space research.

spine out (Of books) displayed on a shelf with the spine facing outwards.

spinner A revolving stand for displaying products for sale.

spiral binding See **mechanical binding.**

split run The printing of the same magazine in two or more separate parts, so that different advertisements can be put into each run. Split runs are used in comparing the different effects and results of magazines containing alternative advertisements.

sponsorship (1) The undertaking of the financial responsibility of a product or project, e.g. a sports competition or series of concerts, often as a form of advertising. (2) (*US*) The payment by a company of the costs of a television or radio programme on which its products are advertised.

spot A single broadcast of an advertisement on television or radio in a unit of advertising time.

spread Two facing pages in a magazine. See also **centre spread.**

Standard Industrial Classification The standard decimal classification and coding of industries and products. Economic activities are divided into ten broad divisions, each given a single digit from 0 to 9, e.g. 1 standing for energy and water supply industries. The divisions are then subdivided into classes (by adding a second digit, e.g. 14 for mineral oil processing). The classes are then further subdivided into additional groups, then activities, each new stage being given an extra digit. Also *SIC*.

standard of living The level of a person's material well-being. It is determined by the quantities, qualities, and range of products and services that he or she is able to buy, which in turn depends upon the disposable income and the availability and prices of the products and services required.

staple product An essential product; one that is bought regularly and in a routine manner. Examples of staple products are milk and bread.

stars Profitable products that have a high market share and a high rate of growth. See also **growth-share matrix.**

static market A market that is generally free from fluctuations or growth or decline over a period of time.

status symbol A possession that shows one's wealth, social importance, prestige, etc.

sticker An adhesive label, poster, or other piece of paper, etc., that can be stuck on a window, counter, or other surface for promotional purposes.

stock Supplies of materials, equipment, or products for sale or for use in manufacture.

stock control Making sure that there is always enough stock available for the production processes, etc., and arranging for the efficient and regular replacement of stock as it is used up.

stockist A dealer in a particular range of goods from a certain manufacturer or supplier.

stocktaking The counting of stock in order to arrive at an estimate of the total value of stocks held. Stocktaking can be done annually, six monthly, etc., depending upon the requirements of the organisation.

store audit See **retail audit.**

storyboard A series of drawings that present the most important elements of a commercial for television or cinema.

strategic business unit   An independent division of a company, especially one with the responsibility for planning the marketing of one of the important product ranges of a company. Also *SBU*.

stratification   The application of rules to the selection of samples so that the samples are representative of the whole population.

structured   (Of an interview) containing solely a set of standard questions, to which direct answers ('Yes', 'No', or 'Don't know') are required.

subliminal advertising   Advertising on television or the cinema, directed to the subconscious, that is shown too rapidly and briefly to make a conscious impression on the viewer. Such advertising is illegal in the UK.

subscribe   (1) To pay for a magazine or newspaper to be received regularly, the amount of money charged being known as the *subscription*.   (2) To place an advance order for a new product, e.g. books before they are published, the level of such orders being known as the *subscription*.

subsidy   Financial support given by the government or a larger company to a firm, industry, or region in order to prevent its decline, to avoid an increase in the price of its products, or to enable its exports to compete more effectively on the international market.

subsistence   The minimum level of provision of food, clothing, and shelter that is necessary to ensure survival.

substitute goods   Two commodities, such as butter and margarine, which are fairly good substitutes for one another because they perform a similar function or serve a similar taste. A rise in the price of one causes some degree of changeover to the substitute.

supermarket   A large self-service store (with a selling area of between 2000 and 25,000 sq ft) in which food and household items, especially those constantly demanded, may be purchased. Supermarkets have several checkouts and usually belong to a chain.

supersite   A large outdoor poster site, often with painted panels.

superstore   A very large single-storey self-service store, with a selling area of between 25,000 and 50,000 sq ft, that sells food and non-food items, has car-parking facilities, and is usually located on the edge of a town.

supply   The quantity of a product or service that suppliers will offer for sale during a given period in response to a particular price.

supply and demand   See **laws of supply and demand.**

surcharge   A charge over and above the normal price of something, e.g. an extra charge for the price of airline tickets if an increase in fuel costs exceeds a certain amount.

survey   A detailed study of something, e.g. the attitudes of consumers or the opinions of members of the public towards a political party, using sampling techniques.

swatch   A bound collection of small samples of fabrics, inks, etc., showing different colours, materials, textures, etc.

SWOT analysis   A strategic study of a company or organisation, by considering its *s*trengths, *w*eaknesses, *o*pportunities, and *t*hreats. Strengths and weaknesses are internal factors (e.g. good organisational structures, poor cash flow). Opportunities and threats are external factors (e.g. a growing market for a company's products, the danger posed by anti-pollution legislation).

symbol retailer   A member of an independent group (a *symbol group*) of retail grocers (e.g. Spar), chemists, etc., who join together to obtain improved discounts and prices from suppliers.

syndicated research   Marketing research that is carried out by marketing research companies and offered for sale to a number of clients.

systems selling   The selling of a whole system, i.e. a product and a range of benefits, to a customer. For example, a complete computer system (with hardware and associated software and peripherals) may be sold to a business company.

Tt

tabloid A page that is half the size of a broadsheet. The term is commonly used to refer to a newspaper with a format approximately 12 in × 16 in (300 mm × 400 mm) that contains a great deal of photographic material.

tabulation The grouping of data into tables for further assessment and evaluation.

tachistoscope A marketing research device that flashes visual presentations of a package, advertisement, etc., for different periods of time; used to measure how effective a design, name, etc., is.

target audience The group of people that an advertising, marketing, etc., effort is aimed at.

Target Group Index Syndicated research carried out by the British Market Research Bureau. The index is based on data from questionnaires completed by over 24,000 adults a year who describe their use of products and brands, viewing habits, etc. Also *TGI*.

target marketing The choosing of one or more market segments on which to concentrate a company's marketing.

tariff (1) Customs duty. (2) A list of goods liable to, and exempt from, customs duty. (3) A list of prices for products or services.

task method A way in which the budget of a promotional activity is calculated: by basing it on the clearly defined goals of the promotion and the desired mix of the promotional elements.

tear sheet   An advertisement torn out of a particular issue of a publication and sent to an advertiser as proof of its publication.

teaser   An advertisement or series of advertisements intended to generate interest by arousing curiosity.

technical press   Publications that deal with specialist technical subjects.

technological forecasting   The forecasting of likely future technological developments, including when they may occur and what they might be. Examples of technological forecasting include the **Delphi technique.**

telemarketing   See **telephone selling.**

telephone interviewing   The obtaining of information for market-research purposes by telephoning a selected group of people (as opposed to face-to-face interviews or postal questionnaires).

telephone selling   The process of calling prospective customers by telephone in order to sell them products or services, either by trying to make an appointment or by making a direct sales presentation. Also known as **telemarketing.**

teleshopping   (1) A service in which customers place orders by telephone for products to be delivered.   (2) A service in which customers can order products selected from information screened on a visual display unit or television in their homes.

teletext   Broadcast videotext. Information is carried from a computer to a receiver by radio waves where pages of information are displayed on a screen, the screen capable of being changed by a push-button selection device. The two systems of this type in operation in the UK are *Céefax* (British Broadcasting Corporation) and *Oracle* (Independent Broadcasting Authority).

television ratings The measurement of the audience of a television programme, based on survey research. The coverage of an advertisement campaign is measured in terms of its television ratings (*TVRs*), one TVR standing for 1% of a defined audience, e.g. housewives or children, who have the television on during a commercial.

tender An offer to do a job, supply goods, etc., for a certain fixed price. Contracts involving the supply of large numbers of items over a period of time or the carrying-out of major construction/repair work are often 'put out to tender' so that various firms can compete for the contract.

territory See **sales territory.**

test marketing The launching of a new product or service in a representative market to resolve any problem that might occur and to discover if it is worth while launching the product or service nationwide.

testimonial A recommendation about the good quality of and satisfaction gained from a product or service from an expert, a famous person, or a satisfied ordinary person.

text The main written or printed words in an advertisement, newspaper article, etc., in contrast to the headings or illustrations.

TGI Abbreviation of **Target Group Index.**

Thomson Directories Classified telephone directories that give information on a particular area as a guide for personal shopping and general business use.

tie-breaker An additional part of a competition to decide the ultimate winner or winners. For example, many people may have correctly chosen an item in the main part of the competition. The tie-breaker, e.g. the writing of a slogan, will then be used to decide which of these contestants is the winner. The writer of the most apt slogan, etc., will be awarded the prize.

tied house (1) A pub, garage, etc., receiving all of its supplies from one particular brewer, oil company, etc. (2) A house whose tenant may occupy it only as long as he or she is employed by the owner. Tied houses are common in agriculture.

time and motion study See **work study.**

tip in A page that is pasted to the adjoining page, rather than being bound with the other pages.

title The legal right to possess goods or property.

token (1) A round flat piece of plastic or metal used instead of money, e.g. in some vending machines. (2) See **book token; gift voucher.**

trade counter The department in a warehouse, etc., where goods are sold to retailers or tradespeople, plumbers, builders, etc.

trade discount An additional discount given to customers who will in turn sell the products to the general public.

trade fair A large international exhibition for organisations and companies to promote a range of their products and services.

trade-in Something given as part of the payment for something else. For example, a person's car is often used as a trade-in when he or she buys a new car.

trade name (1) A trademark. (2) The name under which a company or individual does business.

trade press Publications that deal with specialist trades or professions, e.g. the medical journal *Lancet.*

trade price The price paid by the retailer or tradesperson to the wholesaler for goods which will eventually be sold (at a higher price) to the public.

trademark Any distinctive word, design, or symbol on a product (or accompanying it) which serves to identify it as the product of a particular firm, setting it apart from rival products. Trademarks can be officially registered to prevent others from using them.

trading down   Selling a cheaper type of product, in order to achieve a greater volume of sales; moving down market.

trading stamps   Stamps, e.g. Green Shield stamps, (or similar vouchers) given to a purchaser of goods. The amount given is in proportion to the value of the goods bought and when a person has collected a suitable number he or she can exchange them for cash or for goods supplied by the trading-stamp company.

trading up   Selling a more expensive type of product in order to increase profits; moving up market.

traffic   (1) The number of customers who enter a store or part of it.   (2) (In some advertising agencies) a department that chases the progress of the flow of work to ensure that schedules are kept to.

traffic count   The counting of the number of pedestrians or vehicles that go past a given point in a particular period of time.

train exhibitions   Exhibitions on trains that can travel to different stations and be visited by interested parties in various locations throughout the country.

transfer lettering   Lettering on the back of a plastic sheet that can be rubbed down onto paper, etc., when preparing artwork.

transportation advertising   Poster advertising in or on the sides of buses, in trains, taxis, at stations, airports, etc. See also **outdoor advertising.**

traveller's cheques   Cheques which can be purchased at home and cashed abroad (at various banks, hotels, shops, etc.) for the amount of foreign currency required. Traveller's cheques are a convenient and safe method of carrying money abroad.

travelling exhibition   A completely mobile exhibition, e.g. in a large coach, or an exhibition train (see **train exhibitions**).

trolley   A small cart with four wheels that is used to hold a customer's shopping in a supermarket.

turnkey operation   A project, usually abroad, that requires a large amount of investment, undertaken by a contractor who is given complete responsibility for the design, construction, etc. When the project is completed, the factory, hospital, etc., is handed over to the owners in a state ready for immediate use.

TVR   Abbreviation of *television rating*; see **television ratings.**

typeface   The printing surface of type in one of a variety of styles.

Uu

unaided recall   See **recall.**

undifferentiated marketing   The marketing of a single product or service to all markets.

unique selling proposition   The concept that a product has a particular distinctive feature that distinguishes it from competitive products. This concept is communicated by advertising. Also *USP*.

unit pricing   A form of pricing in which the price per unit of volume, weight, etc., is shown on a package. The use of unit pricing, e.g. on supermarket shelves, facilitates the easy comparison of competing products.

Universal Product Code   See **bar code.**

universe   The total number of people or items from which a sample is taken for statistical purposes. Also known as **population.**

unprompted response   The spontaneous answering of a question by a respondent without any prompting, help, or guidance.

unstructured interview   An interview, as in marketing research, in which the interviewer has guidelines on the main points that should be covered (rather than a fixed set of questions). The guidelines serve as prompts for the free discussion of a subject.

up market   (Of products and services) at the more expensive, more luxurious, higher-quality end of the market.

UPC   Abbreviation of *Universal Product Code*; see **bar code.**

USP   See **unique selling proposition.**

Vv

value added tax   A tax levied at each stage of production from raw materials through to the point of retail. Each organisation charges the next organisation in the chain of production VAT at the standard rate (15%) on the value they have added. Each of these organisations acts as a tax collector and it is required that VAT returns are submitted periodically to the Inland Revenue. Also *VAT*.

value analysis   The systematic checking of the separate elements of a manufactured product to ensure that each element is most efficiently contributing to satisfying the needs of consumers at the lowest possible cost.

van sales   Sales of a selection of a particular type of product, e.g. electrical goods, by a salesperson who drives to different retailers or small businesses and sells the items from the van.

variable   A quantity that can assume any of a set of values. The value of an independent variable determines that of the dependent variable.

variable costs   Costs that change directly as the level of output changes, rising as more is produced and falling as less is produced. These include the costs of materials and power, and of labour that is employed as needed.

variety chain store   A retail shop that sells a wide range of products, especially those with a low unit value.

variety reduction   Cutting down the number of different products or rationalising design, manufacture, or production in the interests of greater profitability.

VAT Abbreviation of **value added tax.**

vending machine An automatic machine that dispenses a product, e.g. a packet of chocolates, a hot drink, a video, or a meal cooked by a microwave, when the specified money is inserted.

vendor The person who sells.

vertical circulation A publication aimed at a readership at all levels of a particular trade or industry.

vertical integration A situation in which a company merges with (or takes over) another company which is involved in a different stage of production or distribution. An iron and steel company which owns mines, foundries, rolling mills, and finished-goods factories is an example of vertical integration.

vertical marketing The development of new markets, in contrast to developing existing ones (*horizontal marketing*).

visual A sketch that shows the rough layout of an advertisement or other promotional material.

visualiser An artist or designer, especially in an advertising agency, who produces roughs or visuals that express the ideas of a brief.

voice-over The spoken commentary to an advertisement on television or cinema, spoken by someone who is not seen.

volume discount A reduction in the unit price of goods when large quantities are purchased.

voluntary chain A group of independent retailers who buy their stock from one wholesaler, so reducing costs and increasing profitability.

voucher (1) A document that is proof of an expense having been incurred. (2) See **gift voucher; luncheon voucher.**

Ww

want Desire to own a product or service.

warehouse A large room or building in which goods are stored, usually in bulk, e.g. by a wholesaler.

warranty An undertaking, generally in writing, guaranteeing that products sold are fit for use, of a stipulated quality, etc., and stating the manufacturer's responsibility to repair or replace the products should they prove faulty (or become faulty within a stated period of time).

wear and tear Damage that comes about by normal use, not covered by warranty.

weighting The attaching of more or less importance to something in order to make it comparable in a more realistic way with others.

Which? A magazine which conducts investigations and surveys into a wide range of consumer products. It is published monthly and aims at unbiased non-political recording and reporting of facts and figures for the general public.

white goods Household appliances such as washing-machines and refrigerators. The expression derives from the time when the surface of these consumer durables was white enamel paint.

wholesaler A trader who buys products in bulk from manufacturers in order to sell them again in smaller quantities, especially to retailers.

wildcats See **problem children.**

window dressing   The structured display of products in a shop window in order to attract customers.

wire binding   See **mechanical binding.**

word-of-mouth   Of advertising in which satisfied consumers tell their relatives, friends, etc., about a product.

work study   The analysis of how jobs are done and the measurement of the time taken to do them, carried out in order to increase efficiency and productivity and to establish standard levels of performance against which an individual worker's performance may be measured. Also known as **time and motion study.**

Yy

year-books Reference books published annually, giving up-to-date information and statistics. A wide range of classifications are covered: business and finance (home and overseas), economics, people, travel, shipping and import/export, technical, scientific, and general reference.

Yellow Pages® A special telephone directory with business subscribers' names and numbers arranged under trade or other social classifications and then alphabetically within the classification. The directory is printed on yellow pages and has many display and semi-display advertisements.

Zz

zero-rating　The rate of value added tax (VAT) applied to specific categories of goods, e.g. food, water, and children's clothing. The rate is zero which means that the consumer pays no tax. Unlike the supplier of exempt goods and services, the supplier of zero-rated goods is entitled to reclaim VAT that he or she has paid on his or her expenses.

zip code　The American equivalent of the British postcode, consisting of a five-figure code for each locality.

Chambers *Commerce Series*

Marketing

Richard J. Watson

Marketing covers the course requirements for the
BTEC National Diploma (option module) and
Higher National Certificate and the Institute of
Marketing Certificate. The book is also suitable
for a wide range of business and training courses
that contain an element of marketing, including
BTEC, CAM, Institute of Purchasing and Supply,
Institute of Export and SCOTVEC. It also serves
as an introduction to marketing for small business
enterprise schemes.

- **SIMPLE, READILY UNDERSTOOD
  LAYOUT**

- **HELPFUL JARGON-FREE LANGUAGE**

- **FREQUENT SELF-ASSESSMENT
  QUESTIONS**

Chambers *Commerce Series*

The up-to-date series for school and college students, embracing the full range of business and vocational subjects.

Business Studies
Mark Juby

A comprehensive introduction to all aspects of business activity. The book covers the GCSE National Criteria in Business Studies, plus key areas of GCSE Commerce and Understanding Industrial Society courses. *Business Studies* is also geared to BTEC, LCCI, O/Standard Grade, RSA and SCOTVEC Courses.

Bookkeeping and Accounting
Harold Randall and David Beckwith

A comprehensive introduction, showing how financial records are made, maintained and used in business. The book is of especial value to students on AAT, BTEC, GCSE, LCCI, PEI, RSA and SCOTVEC syllabuses.

Typing
June Rowley

An introduction to basic typing theory and practice, ideal for a wide variety of secretarial and vocational courses including BTEC, CPVE, GCSE, LCCI, PEI, RSA and SCOTVEC.

Word Processing
Barbara Shaw

Covers everything from text editing to repagination and mail merge—all the practical word processing skills. Ideal for BTEC, LCCI, PEI, RSA and SCOTVEC courses.

Chambers *Commerce Series*

Business Calculations
David Browning

A step-by-step guide to mathematics in business practice, from simple arithmetic to elementary statistics. Geared to courses of many varieties—CPVE, BTEC, LCCI, RSA and SCOTVEC; GCSE and O/Standard Grade Mathematics, professional training.

Business Law
Janice Elliot Montague

A practical introduction to the law, how it works and influences business procedures. *Business Law* covers relevant components of a host of syllabuses—ATT, ALS, BTEC, ICA, ICAS, ICMA, ILE, IOB, IPS, LCCI, SCCA, SCOTVEC.

The Business of Government
J. Denis Derbyshire

A straightforward introduction to British government, how it works in practice and how it influences business procedures. Covers key elements of Politics and Public Administration syllabuses, including BTEC, GCSE, RSA, O/Standard Grade, Modern Studies, SCOTVEC; an ideal reference text for A Level and Higher Grade courses.

Keyboarding
Derek Stananought

A book of exercises and advice on the skills needed in the age of new technology and the electronic office. Includes training material in basic keyboarding, proofreading, speed development, practical application of typing techniques. Ideal for secretarial and vocational courses—BTEC, CPVE, LCCI, PEI, RSA, SCOTVEC.

Secretarial Duties
Penny Anson

A complete guide to all the practical aspects of a
professional secretary's work. Covers the syllabuses of
the important courses, including BTEC, CPVE, LCCI,
PEI, RSA, SCOTVEC.

Office Procedures
Ruth Martindale

A straightforward explanation of the work involved in
running a modern office. Well illustrated, up-to-date,
takes full account of the latest technology and
procedures. Covers the syllabus requirements of BTEC,
LCCI, Pitman, RSA, SCOTVEC.

Business Communication
Gordon Lord

A straightforward introduction to the different forms
of communication used at work. Ideal for Business and
Secretarial Studies courses including CPVE, BTEC,
RSA, LCCI, PEI and SCOTVEC.

Reception Duties
Betty Lowe

A clear introduction to the varied responsibilities of the
receptionist. Written for the RSA Diploma in General
Reception Duties and the BTEC First Award option
module but also ideal for other introductory secretarial
courses.